MW01035306

First Edition: November 2017

ISBN-13: 978-1976363498

ISBN-10: 1976363497

Dedication

I dedicate this book to my mother, Francine Hardin. Even in your failing health you continue to love, inspire and motivate me to become great. I know you are proud of me Momma. I do this for you. I love you.

To Grandma Rose Harris, woman I miss you. You have given me a treasure full of gems I still carry with me today. Although you were tough on me at times, I understand it was out of love. I love you.

To Grandma Annette Sullivan, woman, I know you have been watching over me. My eyelids flood with joyful tears when I think of you. Your compassion and kindness you bestowed within me to always look for the good; even in bad people. I miss you. I love you.

Acknowledgements

First and foremost, I would like to thank GOD because without Him none of this would be possible. His mercy. His grace. His unconditional love has been overwhelming. To my wonderful family and friends, I appreciate your love and support; it means the world to me. I love y'all! To the creative gods that flow within me I thank you for steering my visions. It took me 9 years to write this book. I am grateful and humble. It's a blessing to still be here and share my story. Life at times can be unkind, but it also can be beautiful. I believe sometimes you have to lose yourself in order to find yourself. Many times I had to pick myself up off the ground and no matter how many times I tumbled I thank GOD I had the strength and courage to get back up.

If we start looking beyond what is visible to see what is possible we will understand our events of our yesterdays will strengthen us for the journey of today. I learned time is an important element, once dispensed it cannot be recouped. Use your time wisely, because you never know how much you have left. To Chi-city who birthed me and A-town who raised me, "ONE LOVE!"
To the guys…Cutch, Toby, Marv W, Bo, Quee, Slick, Shinny, KC, Duran, Gerald, Pete, William, Tim, Marvin, MG, C Hunt, Mo, TEO, Walt, Nate, Cee Cee, Deon, Gip, Dre , SP, Dino, Jimmy, JT, Tone, Ronnie, Lawrence, Jerome, Buck, Fred, Vic, Kirk, DD, Sean, Twann, James, Dave, Mr. Mayor, Quick, Duck, Rod, Kevin, Kenny, Cory,V West, Derrick, Keith, Chris M, Mike, Chris, Carl T., Eastside, Westside, Atown.

Thank you and much love to my team; Jocelyn 'Queen' for all you do. Khalilah 'KJ' and Kesha, excellent job at making my book covers look outstanding, Laticha Henry, my editor, and S.O.T on the legwork. To the book clubs who support my work faithfully "Universal Sisters" and "Ain't that the Truth." I appreciate your support. Much Love.

To my brothers, I SAY THIS IN LOVE! You are incredibly blessed with immense talent. However, it's up to you to find it. Once you identify your talent have faith it will lead you to your passion. The most powerful tool you can use is yourself. People will size you up in 3 seconds. But don't stress, remember what you want will come to you if you are clear in the mind and pure in desire.

****

No matter how dark it gets. No matter how hard the pouring black rain falls. As long as you have air to breathe you fight to live another day.

-J. L.

****

Black Rain

Outside My

Window

J.L. Harris

INTRO

When I first sat down to write this book, I must admit I was a bit skeptical. I found myself treading lightly in unfamiliar chartered waters. Thinking how I could write something positive that would perhaps have an influential impact on someone else's life. More importantly my own son's life so he could get a better understanding of who his father is and the extreme measures of turbulence I had to sustain to become the man I am today.

Normally, I am accustomed to writing contemporary fictional tales. I enjoy creating those, but something delving deep inside of me was vexing away at my soul, and convinced me to share my compelling life story with the entire world. I figured all the pain and travesty I had endured and overcame, why not share it? It's one thing to go through pain but it's another thing when your pain is self-inflicted. Those wounds are the hardest to heal.

All I ever wanted to be in life was successful, but I never saw the Black Rain coming. Here's my story.

BLACK RAIN

In my window I sit alone staring out at the unknown as huge black rain drops fell from the murky skies.

The birds of the air couldn't fly high.

People ran for shelter fast as they could, the stiff wind howled like a wolf in the wild.

Doors shook, windows rattled.

The rhythm of the black rain rat-tat tatted on my rooftop like machine gunfire.

Motionless I sat as I watched like a hawk. But, if I sat too long I felt I may drown in my own thoughts.

Like a bad dream black rain seems to haunt me and the ones who look just like me.

In the pouring rain, I see tears of fear.

A mask of soft steel can't pretend to be real.

A rain that cuts so deep, is hard to heal.

No one hears the crackling sound in my voice, nor do they care.

Black rain will kiss you cold and leave you in despair.

PROLOGUE

"We the jury, find the defendant guilty."

"Guilty?" I said inwardly in disbelief. How? The prosecutor's whole case was built on the testimony of a crack-head who perjured to get a favorable deal to save himself. He gave numerous inconsistent statements. *You idiots can't you see through this bullshit*! I wanted to scream. God, I couldn't believe this was happening. I could feel myself starting to panic inside, because a guilty verdict meant I was going away on a long horrible vacation and not by choice.

Truth is; I was starting to realize you never fully understand a situation until your feet are the ones being held over the fire. Anger was an understatement. I was burning hot coals of lava within and I had no one to blame but myself. If I could've kicked myself in the seat of my own pants, I probably would not have been able to sit for a whole week. I allowed these people to do to me as they wish. My mother always told me a hard head makes a soft ass. Just as I thought I was free on the inside, those old festering demons were beginning to resurface. The man I was trying to run away from was suddenly back knocking on my door.

Remarkably I somehow managed to keep my outer being in check long enough for them to usher me out of the courtroom. Trust me it wasn't easy. My attorney was talking fast, whispering in my ear. She could've been talking Chinese for all I cared. I was not trying to hear her. The bailiff slapped the handcuffs back on me and my knees began to quake. This was not good. I could feel my heart racing ready to burst through my chest. They proceeded to escort me out the courtroom and that's when everything began to move in slow motion. The judge's cold eyes spoke volumes. This was just another day at the office for her. She was so much of a coward. She couldn't even look me in the eyes my entire trial. The prosecution team wore hidden grins; the two of them reminded me of Laurel and Hardy. As I shuffled passed them they gave each other high fives and pats on the back, as if this was a championship game and they had just won the trophy.

The world that I once knew was gone and there was not a damn thing I could do about it. All I kept thinking about was my 7-year-old son. I had failed him. Tears stung my eye slits, but I refused to let them fall. I would not give them the satisfaction of seeing me break down like some car on the freeway. If I could've made myself disappear this would've been a good time to have pulled a Houdini. *Lord, help me*!

AHH! THE 70'S

It was a hot Chicago summer night and the air was sticky and thick. I was having a hard time falling asleep. Especially when there were grownups outside my bedroom door having themselves a good time. So I climbed my 5-year-old frame out of the bed and cracked open the door. Now mind you I wasn't your average 5-year-old. I was very inquisitive and I always found myself getting into something I had no business getting into. My uncle Glenn Harris often told me I was the chosen one in the family. I never knew what he meant by that. But as I got older those same words he spoke would come back and give me an eye opening revelation.

I peeked my head outside the door and immediately I could hear the smooth soulful sounds of Al Green's 'Love and Happiness' coming from the back porch. Almost every weekend my uncles Dennis, Maurice and Glenn, and a host of their friends drank and partied into the wee hours of the night. Sometimes arguments and fights broke out, but nevertheless, they would make up and be back at it again the very next weekend like nothing had ever happen.

As a 5-year-old, my eyes witnessed more than I needed to see. I learned about the birds and the bees watching my uncle Glenn sneak girls into the room we shared. With one eye open and pretending to be asleep, I found out girls had the real candy. Grown-ups called it sex, kids we called it juicing. My uncle Glenn was a smooth cat, always singing and laughing, he was a joy to be around. So I gravitated towards him as much as I could.

We originated from the Robert Taylor Homes, 4410 South State Street, that's the first home I knew. But after my mother and father couldn't make it work, my mom, Sister Twanda and me moved in with our Grandmother. Grandma Rose Harris lived off of 43rd street and Prairie on the South Side of the City. Two years later my mother would give birth to a third child named Tiffany. I was the middle child and for the most part my early childhood was exciting. However, it didn't take long for me to figure out we were poor. Don't get me wrong I think we had what we needed. We just didn't have enough of what we wanted.

I had a friend named Keith and he had a sister named Star, they lived in the next building. I spent most of my time over at their apartment playing with all of Keith's plenitude of toys. He had everything I wish I had as a kid. I remember one Christmas we both wanted a Green Machine. They were these new big wheel toys that every kid wanted. But I don't think any kid wanted one more than me. On Christmas day I woke up bright and early but I didn't see a Green Machine under the tree. I was devastated when my mother handed me a Muhammad Ali boxing game. I loved Ali, he was my champ, but where was my Green Machine? Santa Claus gave Keith one, but not me. As soon as the weather broke Keith rode his Green Machine like it was a brand new Cadillac. Every time I would ask if

I could ride he would often say his mother told him he couldn't let, nobody ride it.

Needless to say I was not a happy camper. He knew how bad I wanted a Green Machine for Christmas because we talked about it every day all day, now I was the one still stuck riding my old yellow big wheel. I asked my Grandma, why Santa Claus didn't bring me a Green Machine. She said, "Boy, Santa didn't bring me one either." I looked at her dumbfounded as she chewed on a sweet Peach. The cold look she gave me I can still see today.

That was the last time I ever asked Santa Claus for anything. I started putting two and two together and Santa Claus wasn't adding up. We lived on the third floor, we had no chimney and how was an old fat white man going to deliver presents to all the kids around the world in the middle of the night? He was phony like the tooth fairy. I knew he wasn't real because I saw Grandma Rose take my tooth from underneath my pillow and replace it with two quarters. As a kid I learned things on the fly, and everything grown-ups told you wasn't always the truth.

One afternoon I was sitting on our third floor porch bored looking at Keith and his fat cousin Chris. They were taking turns riding Keith's Green Machine. Every so often they would gaze up at me and quickly look away and snicker. Seconds later my grandmother walked out on the back porch and she peeped the frown on my face. “Boy why you ain’t downstairs playing?’ She asked. With tears stinging my eyes. “They won’t let me ride,” I replied.

“So what you got your own big wheel,” She said coldly.

I didn’t say anything I just shrugged it off, because Grandma Rose could be feisty at times. Although she was small in stature she was tough as a nail. Everybody called her Red because of her fair light skin tone. Sometimes they would jokingly call her nosey-rosey. But make no mistake my Grandma was nothing to play with. Hands down, she was the toughest woman I knew and when she wanted to, she could easily raise some hell. I watched her take broom sticks pots and pans and try and break them over people heads.

“Well, what you going to do boy keep sitting there?” She asked placing her hands on her hips.

I sighed heavily and reluctantly grabbed my old big wheel and dragged it down the stairs. The last thing I wanted to do was ride that old raggedy thang. As soon as I came down those stairs Fat Chris started roasting me. “Aye Keith, look who didn’t get a Green Machine,” he laughed.

I looked over at Keith and he had a goofy grin on his dark hue face. Now I really didn’t care too much for Fat Chris; he was nothing more than a bully. He was like 8, but looked like he was 12. He easily outweighed every kid on the block. Personally I didn’t like him because every time he came around he would pick on me.

Name-calling, teasing, and he was always trying to fight me. As a kid I wasn't too much of a fighter. I was a thinker and I liked to get along with everyone. But it didn't take long to realize every one didn't think like me.

I paid Fat Chris no mind and got on my big wheel. As I rode pass him he kicked my back wheel. "Aye, keep your feet on the ground!" I yelled at him.

Oh boy I should've kept my big mouth shut because he began running after me. My poor little feet couldn't petal fast enough, he was all over me like a bad nightmare. I tried to shake him off of me, but fat boy wasn't going. The next thing I knew I was being pummeled and his fist felt like tiny stones hitting me. I was far from a fighter so best thing I could do was try to cover my face; something I always seen Muhammad Ali do when he was in trouble in the ring. This went on for several minutes but felt like hours. Suddenly, out of nowhere I could hear my grandmother's voice. "Boy get up right now," she yelled.

When I looked up she was standing on the porch beaming down on me. Fat Chris paused enough to let me up. I didn't care what she was talking about I didn't want no parts of him. I bolted right upstairs and left my big wheel for dead. As soon as I got upstairs grandma Rose was angry and I couldn't understand why? I'm the one who just got the beating of my life.

"Boy get back downstairs and hit him back you don't let nobody put their hands on you. Now go!" She ordered.

I couldn't believe she wanted me to go back down there and get killed. I pleaded with her as tears spilled out my eyelids. The last thing I wanted to do was dance with the devil again. This was not a good time in my young life. "Grandma I don't want to fight," I sobbed.

"Boy if you don't get back down there and fight, I'm going to give you something to cry for. We ain't raising no sissies!"

I knew what that meant. So basically, I was in a pickle with no room to wiggle. Grudgingly, I walked my way back down to a death I knew was coming. At this time a few more bystanders came to witness the massacre. Fat Chris fists were already cocked and loaded. I put my head down and charged screaming like my hair was on fire. I didn't quite know why I was screaming but it felt good. Something I saw Bruce Lee do when he went in to battle.

Moments later, my grandmother was pulling the beast off of me. "Win or lose, you fight boy, you hear me."

"Yes ma'am," I replied, wiping hot tears from my moist cheeks.

For years I resented my grandmother for some of the hard lessons she gave that had a negative impact on me as a child. Being called "Boy," instead of my name, Jerald was insulting. For years I thought my name was Boy and my worth didn't have any value. I knew she loved me, but sometimes I thought she had a funny way of showing it. But as I grew older I understood the unharmonious lessons. She only taught me what she knew and her gems of wisdom were priceless. A young boy just wants to go outside and play and have fun, he's not thinking that someone may want to hurt him.

Grandma Rose was preparing me for the black rain that was coming my way. The hate. The injustice. Black on Black crime. The police brutality. The racism. The drugs. The gangs. The impoverishment. If you didn't have the essential tools to survive, you were not going to make it. She always told me to be strong. When you're a young boy you don't know what strong is. But I thank God for her; she was a blessing.

Later that evening my uncle Maurice came to talk to me. Now Maurice was cool and really easy to talk too. He always kept a clean car and some money in his pocket. He would often take me for rides. One of my favorite spots to go was the gas station. I just loved the way gas smelled, it was a high that always put a smile on my face. Plus he would buy me a bag of salt and sour potato chips. Even to this day, I still love salt and sour potato chips.

In my young eyes, my uncle Maurice was the man I wanted to be like when I got older. He was kind, understanding, and he was a lot of fun to be around. He told me, "Don't worry about a big wheel! One day you gonna have nice big cars and them boys still are going to be riding big wheels!" After he gave me a little pep talk, I felt like I was floating on clouds. I never did think about a Green Machine again. The seed my uncle Maurice planted taught me to think bigger. Don't want what everybody else wants. Be different make them want what you have.

Growing up on the South Side of Chicago was definitely challenging even for a kid my age. Everything moved at an expeditious pace. At 6 years old, I was learning to hustle. Doing whatever I could to get money. Returning pop bottles and helping old ladies with their shopping bags. I learned to build go-carts and sling shot guns.

Literary it took a village to raise child. The neighborhood always stood together and everyone always looked out for each other. Was it perfect? No! But we were like family. However, one thing I didn't like is if you got in trouble outside of the home, the neighbor down the street would give you a whooping. Then they would take you home and tell your parents what happened, and then you would get another whooping! I wasn't down with this program so I learned at an early age if you are doing wrong, you better not get caught.

One of my favorite spots on 47th street was Queen of the Sea. Man they had a big bag of barbeque fries to kill for. The smell of the hustle and bustle on the block was enticing. I'd seen everything from pimps, players and hustlers. Even knew a few Black Panthers. It was a great time to be alive you would often see cats on the street corners harmonizing melodies. I saw Chicago as a big ocean and if you couldn't swim you will drown.

The very next summer Uncle Maurice drove Grandma Rose and me down south to Montgomery, Alabama, which is located on the Alabama River, in the Gulf Coastal Plain. The ride seemed like it took us forever. This was my grandmother's hometown and her entire family was here. As I sat in the back seat, the blazing sun sat right next to me. I couldn't believe how hot it was, this was crazy. Suddenly I found myself missing Chicago. The heat was unbearable. Our first stop was at my grandmother oldest sister's house Ellen Gertrude Baily better known as Big Mama. Big Mama lived in a yellow house on Auburn Street with a small back yard. Everything was neat and clean. When it came down to cooking the house smelled just like a restaurant.

Big Mama was a delightful woman; she had a good sense of humor and she loved to do for others. Every mourning she would cook eggs, grits, bacon, and biscuits. Never in my young life had I seen so much food. However, I wasn't feeling the country life. It was too doggone hot and big bugs were all over the place. I couldn't wait to get back home to the South Side of Chicago, I felt completely out of my elements. Big Mama sensed I was uncomfortable. She gave me a bowl of ice cream and we sat out on the porch. I was thanking God the burning sun had finally gone down. This woman was remarkable and her infectious laughter always brought smiles. She gave me the rundown on the ins and out about Montgomery,

Alabama. I learned about the civil rights movement and about Dr. King and Rosa Parks, and the bus boycott. She was very informative and like a good student I soaked up everything like a sponge.

At the time, I was too young to understand the significance of our conversation. Of course as I got older, the history lesson Big Mama had given me turned out to be priceless.

Then we visited Pinkie Powell, my Grandmother Rose's mother. We stayed at her house during our stay. We called her Granny Annie. She was tiny and at times she could be mean. She believed in discipline and respect. If you did wrong, she was notorious at making you go get a switch from a tree and tear you a new one. This woman spoke her mind and could care less if you didn't like it. Now I could see where Grandma Rose got her toughness from, her Mama! And my mother wasn't too far from them.

After a couple weeks had a passed, we said our goodbyes to the many friends and cousins that I had met. Some of the younger kids kept referring to Grandma Rose as Aunt Candy. I thought that was strange because I never heard that before. I watched as the kids joyfully gathered around Aunt Candy. She gave them all big hugs and kisses. As we were leaving I could tell my Grandma Rose was kind of sad because her eyes were misty. "Grandma why they call you Aunt Candy?" I inquired once inside the car.

"Boy I'm more than just a Grandma! Now sit back we got a long ride ahead of us," she chuckled. I beamed brightly as her hand brushed through my short crop hair. The only thing that mattered to me was that we were headed back home to Chicago, because the blazing sun had already baked my skin like hot bread in an oven. Sadly, that was last time I ever saw Big Momma. But I was sure glad she slipped me them homemade sugar cookies. Needless to say, I had a huge Kool-Aid smile plastered all over my face on the long drive back home.

Finally, we made it back home and boy was I happy to see the Sears Tower lingering in the distant. As a kid I loved traveling in a car gazing out the window enjoying everything I saw. I was amazed on how everything moved; cars, buses, trains, airplanes and trucks. The 70's, in my little eyes, were a great time to be alive and I cherished every moment. I was learning about life and all it had to offer. I wanted to conquer this thing they called life. It was beautiful!

WHAT'S GOING ON

The sound of loud thunder woke me up early on a Saturday morning. I hated thunder! It always scared the living hell out of me. I cautiously tip toed my way down the long narrow hallway that lead into the dining room area. My grandmother's drinking buddy, Blockhead, was drunk fast asleep snoring on the couch. I never knew his real name everybody called him Blockhead. He was an older man that smelled like a walking bottle of Wild Irish Rose. Blockhead was tall and thin, and wore a pair of thick black square bifocals that made him look sort of comical. He had a huge head similar to a block so I could easily see how the name Blockhead was born. I stood over him in disgust; just the smell of this old fart was just awful.

"Boy what are you doing up so early?" Grandma Rose inquired, coming from the kitchen.

"The thunder woke me up Grandma," I replied wiping sleep out my eyes.

I noticed my grandmother was moving slow and she would grimace in pain. She was starting to do that a lot lately. After she went back into her bedroom that was next to the kitchen, I thought I would have a little fun messing with Blockhead. I took off his smelly sock and placed it around his mouth. Yeah I was a bad boy. But this part of my life was fun. Sometimes I would pick pocket his loose change. My uncle Glenn taught me that. He often would say *you gotta be light as a feather.*

Later that afternoon I hung around the house and watched the Cubs game with my uncle Dennis. Dennis was a character within himself. He stood tall at 6 ft. 3 inches slim and yellow, as a banana. He was the live wire out of all my mother brothers. He would get drunk and love to fight. Budweiser was his beer of choice. Sometimes he would get so drunk he would pass out. I remember one morning we had to get ready for school and Dennis was in the bathroom stretched out like a lawn chair. Man I thought he was dead. Grandma Rose tried her best to wake him up, but it was to no avail. We had to squeeze into the bathroom to brush our teeth and wash our face.

When Dennis got drunk you couldn't tell him nothing and as a kid I paid close attention to everything that moved around me. He was fun at times and other times he was difficult to be around. Don't get me wrong I loved him dearly, but sometimes I wished he would've loved himself more instead of Budweiser. You never know what someone's going through. I believe demons are real and Lord knows I myself would encounter them throughout my life.

One year later, I felt the pain of losing a loved one. Grandma Rose got sick and they rushed her back down south to Alabama. A couple weeks later she died from cancer. The family I knew would never be the same again. I came home from school to hear the bad news. Everybody was enraged; it was a madhouse. Our furniture was put outside on to the street everything was chaotic, too much for a 7-year-old brain to grasp. After the misunderstanding of unpaid rent was squashed we were allowed to move our belongings back in, but shortly after Grandma Rose funeral things went from bad to worse.

My uncles and my mother were at war with each other. I witnessed my mother stab my uncle Maurice in the leg blood, was everywhere. I held a screwdriver in my hand ready to help if needed. I thought my mother was unfairly getting a raw deal of being blamed for Grandma Rose's death. The next thing I knew my mother had packed us some clothes and in the middle of the night we left and never returned.

One thing I can say about my mother she was a fighter and did whatever she had to do right or wrong, she always found a way. For months we bounced around until we finally found a place on 60th and Wabash. It was our second place of our own since we lived in the Robert Taylor Homes. Living on 60th and Wabash was actually a lot of fun. We lived right next door to Betsy Ross Elementary School. We didn't have much but at least we had each other and some decent new friends. My grandfather, Elijah Harris was my mother's father. He lived in the building around the corner. He was a mild mannered gentleman who stood tall, smooth and debonair.

My mother thought it would be a great ideal for me to live with my grandfather since we only had a one-bedroom apartment. I thought it would be too, until I burned a hole in his back porch trying to boil eggs. At the time I was 7 years old, hell I didn't know a plastic tall kitchen garbage can could burn through wood. When my granddad woke up and saw what I had done. He was pissed.

I was smart enough to remove the garbage can from the apartment so it wouldn't burn up. But he said it was dumb to just sit it on the back porch he said I should've thrown it over the banister. So to make a long story short my grandfather packed my bag and took me back home to my mother. Of course my mother wasn't trying to hear anything and she beat me like I was a runaway slave. Sometimes I just couldn't win for losing, a pattern I would become familiar with. Although, I loved my mother's side of the family, sometimes I felt alienated and I couldn't wait to go spend time with my father's side of the family.

The far south of Chicago off of 95th and Loomis was where my father, Gerald Sullivan and the Sullivan family resided. Every time I visited, I would often wish I could stay and live there. My Grandmother Annette Sullivan was my lifeline this woman had a heart of gold. Through her eyes I could do no wrong. The greatest advice she ever gave me was, always be the best at what you do, they will never be able to take away your talents. My Grandmother meant the world to me. Any time I ever needed anything, she made sure I had it. She was a kind-hearted woman. Sometimes this woman and I would stay up all night watching old movies and talking our heads off until the sun came up. Man, how I miss those days.

My Grandmother had 6 children, Gerald, Patricia, Julius (Wooky), Janette, Margaret and Phillip. My Grandfather, William Sullivan anchored the household. William Sullivan stood tall at 6'3 inches. He was a gentle man, he didn't say much, but when walked into a room he wore a certain mystique that captivated you. He was a World War II veteran and a proud strong black man. We didn't spend a lot of time together, but when we did it was mostly watching the Chicago Cubs and White Sox baseball games. He was a huge baseball fan, so that's where we connected.

Throughout my childhood I spent almost all my summers with my Dad's side of the family. He came from a big family. Where there were 3 boys and 3 girls. It kind of reminded me of the Brady Bunch except there wasn't any Alice running around. As a kid that's where I had my fondness memories.

My Uncle Phil was my favorite Uncle by far. He was probably one of the smartest person's I knew. The man could fix and build anything with his hands, but as a kid I was more fascinated by his story telling ability. He would tell these off the wall but humorous bedtime stories that would have me almost peeing my pants. It made me into a storyteller and over the years it turned me into a talented writer. I never really had a solid relationship with my father, so my uncles always filled that void. I don't know the reasons for my father's absence, but for the record, I never held it against him. He was there for me when I needed him the most.

Our time on 60th and Wabash was short lived. Soon we were packing up and on the move once again. This time it was to Hyde Park. We moved into a one-bedroom basement apartment on 5210 S. Woodlawn. My sisters and I shared the bedroom; while my mother slept in the front room on a lay out couch. Richard my younger sister's father would still come around. We called him "Mack" He was definitely a ladies man. He drove big cars and wore fancy suits. Overall I liked him. I thought he was a cool cat. He even took us to the Bozo Show.

Times were tough and with my mother working a full time job from 3 to 11 pm it forced us to fend for ourselves. At times, a syrup sandwich became my go to meal. When I got tired of eating them I would go to the store and take what I wanted to eat, from ham to bologna meat, chicken, etc. To me this was the norm you did whatever you had to do to survive. But I loved living in Hyde Park. On any given day Jesse Jackson, Louis Farrakhan, or Muhammad Ali would ride pass, our house. At eight years old, I was in tune with these great leaders and I knew where all of them lived. On many occasions my friend Nick and I would go over to Ali's huge mansion in Kenwood hoping to get a glimpse of the champ. He would always have his Rolls Royce parked in the driveway of his gated estate.

I remembered one particular morning my friends and I were playing hooky from Kozminski Elementary School. Playing a little hooky is something we did often. Being chased by the truant officer was fun. He would chase us all through Hyde Park as we jumped from building to building, hiding on rooftops trying to elude him. For the record we never got caught and I guess that was a good thing, because my mother would've torn a lining out my behind.

One day, we were hanging out on Lake Shore Drive down by the beach. We couldn't believe Ali and his entourage was heading towards us. The Champ was jogging and the first thing he said to us, "Shouldn't you kids be in school." Of course we came up with the quickest lie we could tell. *Our school had no school today.* I was in awe I couldn't believe it I finally had a chance to speak to the Champ. We were probably the happiest bunch of badass kids on the planet. Had I not decided to play hooky that day, I probably would have never got a chance to meet my idol. Although a brief encounter, as I look back that was one of the fondest days of my life.

After we left the beach, we were still pumped about seeing the Champ. So we did what we always did to get money; we stopped by the Museum of Science and Industry on Lake Shore Drive. You may be asking yourself how did we get money at an museum? Well I was the crafty one in the group and the top money earner. I would find a mark and pick pocket his wallet. An elderly man was ideal for a quick come-up. I would accidently bump into them and carefully remove their wallet without being detected.

The Museum of Science and Industry became our number one hustle spot every Saturday. The place would be jammed pack and we knew the place inside and out. We were in places no kids should have been. Stevie, John-John, Pete, and I were like the 4 musketeers. We called ourselves the Woodlawn boys. We all lived on Woodlawn Street except for Pete he lived on Greenwood with his grandmother. Today President Obama's house, sits on that very same street. We also worked for money shoveling snow in the winter and helping elderly women with their groceries bags outside the A & P. Hustling became a must for us. What we didn't have, we did whatever it took to get it. I remembered my mother had found my stash I had hidden in a sock in the bottom draw. It was $73.00 dollars. "Where did you get this money? She asked giving me the, you better not lie to me look.

I swallowed the lump that was in my throat. "I got it hustling and I've been saving it," I replied holding my breath, hoping she wouldn't pop me.

To my surprise her face soften and I watched closely as her fingers revisited the crumple bills. Her mouth moved but no words came out. After she finished counting the money again. A smile cracked her lips. "I need to borrow this momma gone give it back to you."

I was devastated my roads to the riches, was cut short. I never did see that money again. And I never did hid money in a draw again either.

My Hyde Park days were wild, but fun. I remember going to school and not really learning anything. I was in third grade and to be honest I could barely read or write. The two classes I excelled in the most were gym and performing arts. In school, I mostly kept to myself until this one kid started trying to bully me. His name was Dontae and he was a real live wire. I couldn't stand the sight of him. He was bigger than me and black as midnight. He would always call me Cooley High because he thought I resembled Cochise from the movie Cooley High. Of course, the classroom would roar in laughter. He was the clown of the class. "Hey y'all look at Cooley High's cheap shoes," he would point and there would be more laugher.

He would really tease me when the teacher made me read out loud and I would stutter. I would be so embarrassed. I hated coming to school. So one day Mr. Bully decided he was going to go in on me the whole day. I mean the kid talked about me so bad I wanted to crawl in a hole and die. I tried my best not to respond to him and that seemed to really piss this kid off. The next thing I knew he hauled off and punched me dead in my eye. That's when my lights got shut off. Everything turned black and I couldn't see anything but stars. When my vision returned, I was furious. I leaped from my desk with the roar of a lion. The teacher got in between us while the rest of the kids laughed and roared with the oo's and ah's. She made me go sit outside in the hallway and he was the one who hit me.

The very next day Mr. Bully was back and I was getting tired of him. But this time I had a surprise for him. We were out on recess and he approached me at the merry-go-round. I was minding my own business and he pushed me down. I gave him the look of death. One thing Grandma Rose taught me was if you can't beat them, you find something that can. All night long I thought about how I was going to give him some get back. Now mind you, I was a little scrawny kid that had heart but didn't like to fight. So I hid a rusty screwdriver in my pocket and when I got up I pulled it out and chased him like a madman. Let me tell you Mr. Bully never bothered me again. He called ME crazy, image that!

My day of being the man of the house was coming to an end. My mother started dating this guy named Frank that everyone called "Bubba." It didn't take long for him to move in. He and my mother became inseparable. He had a sister Audrey who lived next door who always looked out for us when my mother was away at work. She had a teenage daughter named Vonda. I had mixed feelings about this guy. He stood tall, lean and mean, his skin was dark and he had the presence of a person you definitely didn't want to mess with if push came to shove. I was very protective of my mother. There were times, I would be walking with her and guys would be making catcalls. I would always give them menacing glares. My mother meant the world to me and she was all I had.

However life moved on. As for me I felt like sometimes I was in a world alone. Even when I looked at television I looked at it in another way. The Lone Ranger was a popular T.V. show, but it wasn't my type of show. It always portrayed the white man as the hero. Guys like Tonto were my hero's he was the underdog and without him The Lone Ranger would be nothing.

All my young life I was told, don't trust the white man. You got to work harder than everybody else because you're black and you are a nigger. Nigger? What is a nigger? I was being bombarded with so much information, but I wasn't getting fed the right amount of substance to process it all. So much madness was going on, I was beginning to realize my world wasn't looking so pretty.

One day Bubba and I were riding in the car and we got pulled over by the Chicago Police right outside our apartment building on Woodlawn. This was my first encounter with the police. Calmly Bubba looked me in the eyes and handed me a small plastic bag that looked like it had greenish brown dirt in it. He said, "Put this in your pocket and go give this to your mother. Go!" I leaped from the car if though my named Jesse Owens and ran across the street into our apartment building. "Momma. Momma," I said bursting through the door, "the police got Bubba, he told me to give this to you."

"Where, what happen?"

"Right outside in the front," I told her.

I really didn't know what was going on. As kids we were taught the police were no good and we saw enough evidence to believe it. Bubba was the third man I seen walk into our lives and he was starting to grow on me. Naturally, I became concerned about him. Turned out he didn't have a driver's license and he went to jail. Ease dropping on grown folks' conversation always proved valuable to gather information. Grown folks, I noticed, were notorious at running their mouths.

I found out Bubba did time in prison for arm robbery and he just got out. However, his past didn't seem to bother my mother. She was head over heels in love with him. He was a street hustler. We always had stolen goods in the house. I remember one day he came home with a box full of calculators and other electronics. As a kid I became fascinated, he was an outlaw, and deep inside I knew I was too. I can't explain it, but being an outlaw seemed to be more appealing than a regular Joe.

Franklin "Bubba" Thomas was the new man of the house and he did help provide for us. He had a friend named Shelton. Shelton was his running buddy, turns out they did a bid for arm robbery. At the time these guys were in their late thirties. Shelton was short and stocky with a peanut butter colored skin tone. He had an old lady with two kids living in St. Charles a small suburb of Chicago. I remember the very first time visiting. It was on a weekend and I had never seen so many white folks before. I kept looking for black people, but didn't see any. Shelton introduced us to his family. Delores was his old lady and Cynthia and Darryl were their children.

Darryl and I were close to the same age and my sister Twanda and Cynthia were almost the same age. The three-bedroom townhouse they lived in was huge and they had their own washing machine and a dishwasher. I couldn't believe it! I didn't know any black folks in my world who, lived like this. Everything was so immaculate. I didn't see any roaches or mice traps. They had it made. Everything was so different; even the air smelled different. I could easily see myself living here.

In my eyes Darryl was one lucky kid that didn't appreciate what he had, he always whined about everything. We got along for the most part; even though we both lived in two different worlds. Growing up on the South Side of Chicago was not an easy task. I had to face all kinds of difficult circumstances and challenges he wouldn't know anything about. Eating syrup sandwiches or wishing you had your very own room. But that was my cold reality. It seems like life always had a funny way of slapping me in the face. However, Darryl was very smart and I envied that more than any of the material things he had. I just wished one day too, I could have it all.

CHANGES

One day coming home from school my mother told us we were moving. *Moving? Where? Why?* I couldn't believe we were going to be on the move again. Just when I found some really good friends and a place I could call home. I was hot and I was tired of moving. I contemplated running away, but that didn't happen. On top of that my mother was pregnant and she was getting bigger. Two weeks later, we were all packed up and on our way to Aurora, Illinois.

When we arrived I saw a sign that read Welcome to Aurora the City of Lights population of 81,000. *City of Lights?* I didn't exactly know what that meant, but we were here. Along the strip I was starting to see why they actually called it the city of lights. Everything was lit up like a Christmas tree as we drove down Lake Street. I had never seen so many restaurants and stores on one block all clustered together. We pulled into an apartment complex with two large buildings, one sat at the bottom of a hill. I got out the car and was blown away by my new surroundings. I read the numbers on top of the brick building, 829 it read. I noticed both of the buildings had 6 floors. Our apartment was 1B on the first floor. It was a two bedroom so that meant I would be sleeping on front room couch. Trust and believe I was not a happy camper.

The very next day I woke up bright and early. I heard some kids playing out back. I slid the sheet back we had up for a curtain back and watched the kids play in the snow. They were two black kids then a white kid joined them. I never saw black kids and white kids play together. I thought that was interesting. I couldn't wait to go and check everything out for myself. After we settled in and registered for school, the first friend I met was a white kid named Derrick. We were in the same homeroom 4P, Patterson class, at Goodwin Elementary School in North Aurora.

Derrick lived on the second floor above us with his mother and redhead little brother Jamie. I couldn't believe we had white people living amongst us. It was definitely an eye opener. They were poor like most us and we all for the most part got along. My first day of school was awful I was the only black in my class. I felt so out of place these kids were smart. They were writing in cursive, doing fractions, and other things I knew nothing about. In Chicago, we never learned that. It didn't take long for the teacher, Mr. Patterson, to realize I didn't have the slightest idea of what the hell was going on. Everything moved at a fast pace and I felt like a ship lost at sea. Even the kids talked funny they weren't hip or cool. It took me awhile to adjust to the suburban life style. I did enough in school to keep my head above water. Hands down, I was smart when it came to the streets, but when it came to books I was far from the sharpest knife in the drawer.

My new friend Derrick was pretty cool. He showed me the area and gave me a rundown on who's who and what was what in Aurora. As time progressed we became jam tight and for a white boy that was poor, he shared the same problems black folks had. *How to escape poverty*? Money wasn't falling from the sky so I had to find a hustle. I noticed every time I would walk into a store all eyes would be on me. They would be waiting for me to steal something. So I got hip. I had Derrick take what we needed and I would buy something with loose change. It was so many ways to get money it was sweet as candy. There was a restaurant, named Big Boy, on the corner of Illinois and Lake Street. We would go in there and steal tips off the table. If that didn't work, we collected cans and put a couple of rocks in the bags to get more money. Hustling wasn't, nothing new to me, the streets of Chicago had already prepared me. So this was a walk in the park.

The first black kids I got jammed with were Sean Parker and Kirk Turner. Sean was a year older and definitely a lot wilder. My family and his family became close. My mother and his mother Dorothy were best friends and so were our older sisters. So we became like family. Kirk on the other hand was my ace. We did everything together. When we weren't outside getting into mischief, we would sit and watch the Chicago Cubs religiously like we were in a Sunday morning church service. Baseball was my first love and my dream was to play in the majors. I wanted to be Hank Aaron and Willie Mays.

Months later we had a new member to our family, my brother Frank Thomas was born. Now it was four of us two boys, and two girls. My mother continued to work so we had to look after the little one. My mother didn't play when it came to cleaning HER house. She referred to it as HER house because she paid the bills. If HER house wasn't clean when she came home from work all hell would break loose. Everything had to be spotless. I've been on the end of a lot of those whippings. Francine Harris didn't play when it came to cleaning you either fell in line or you got dealt with.

The 80's were upon us. My mother and Bubba had just got married. Little Frank was walking and the birth of this new music called hip-hop was taking off. The Sugar Hill Gang were hip hopping it and Kurtis Blow was telling us all about "The Breaks." I cannot lie I was starting to get use to the suburban life even though we went back and forth to the City all the time. Chicago will always be home, but living in Aurora I saw more opportunities. My old friends in Chicago would often tease me about living in the 'burbs. It's funny though they would always ask a whole bunch of questions mostly about white girls.

In Aurora I was making new friends, Lonnie, Mike, Eddie, Melvin P, Craig, Kenny, Robert, Jason and Little Freddy. We had good times and there were a few bad times. We all use to hang down by the Fox River. One day, Eddie and Michael's older brother "Dead Eye" had drowned. Dead Eye was definitely a daredevil and to see him lose his life gave me a new outlook on my own life. I had to slow down because I too was living my life in a reckless abandonment matter. We were not super heroes. This was a wakeup call for us all realizing that life can be taken at any moment.

Weeks later the word death would hit home again even harder. My uncle Glenn Brown Harris was found shot to death. Words are indescribable the pain I felt in my young heart. My uncle had a beautiful soul full of life and energy. His larger than life smile made you want to smile. I was starting to get numb to the word death. It was like a cold slap in the face that never left your soul. I couldn't believe somebody would want to shot and kill my uncle. He was a cool cat that got along with everyone always laughing and playing.

First Grandma Rose now Glenn, I was starting to see the world for what it was and the ice made it too cold. Later we found out my uncle was gambling, playing cards and won big. The guy wanted his money back my uncle refused the guy shot him in chest. Instantly his life was taken. We grieved then life moved on. However the pain never leaves, it lessens but it still aches sometimes when you touch it.

Finally we moved into a three-bedroom apartment on the second floor of our building and I had a bedroom I could finally call my own. This was the same apartment my friend Derrick lived in before they moved. I was delighted and it made me appreciate the small things in life. The apartment was more spacious it even came with a balcony that over looked the front of the building. Bubba had a son named Dinarr; we called him Pussycat. He came to visit us from Chicago a few times, and let me tell you Dinarr was something else. He was a short version of his old man and he loved to get in mischief. What I did like about Pussycat was he had a lot of heart and would scrap on demand.

The first fight was with a kid named Morris. Morris and I were arguing. He called my mother a bitch and all hell broke loose. Pussycat jumped off of my bike and we double-teamed Morris and he ended up having an asthma attack. After the smoke, had settled Morris and I became cool, we had respect for one another. His younger brother, Cory and I later would become good friends. Cory had a younger sister named Melinda. She was a tomboy and she stuck to us like glue. For a girl she was pretty good at playing basketball. Ever chance we got we tried to make it tough on her on the court. But to her credit Melinda was tougher than we thought she didn't back down. Later she would become one the greatest female basketball players in Illinois of all time.

Lake Street Apartments wasn't a bad place to live, some of the friend's I met there we are still good friends to this day. In the back of our building was a basketball court and I use to watch the older kids come out and play. This one slim kid used to live on our floor at the end of the hall. His name was Randy Norman. Randy would shoot and dribble that ball all over the complex. I used to marvel at the way he could shoot and the next thing I knew I wanted to play basketball every day. Playing basketball became my new adventure and I loved it, even though I wasn't that good.

Living in Lake Street Apartments I did have my fair share of fights. This tiny little kid named Lester hit me with a rock one day so I picked up a coke bottle and began chasing him. His father ran down the stairs and stopped me just in the nick of time as I was getting ready to bust his son's head wide open. "Boy who in the hell you think you gonna hit with that bottle?" he yelled snatching the bottle from my hand.

"Him," I said defiantly, "He hit me with a rock."

The man leered at me. "Boy this is my son! Little nigger you ain't going to do shit to him."

I took two steps back and I eyed the man cautiously. The vulgar language didn't scare me and the short little man didn't frighten me. I was from the South Side of Chicago. I had seen and heard far worse. I told him I was going to get my father.

"Go get him," he yelled and began following me.

The man and his boy Lester followed me back down to our building. I was moving at a fast pace. I couldn't wait for Bubba to rip this fool apart. *I'll show him.* When we reached my apartment 2A, the man still had the look of steel on his face. As long as I live I will never forget the look on the man's face when Bubba open that door.

"What's going on?" Bubba asked.

Before I could get a word out the man quickly had a change of heart. “Aw what’s up Frank? I didn’t know this was your son,” he said in a respectful tone. I couldn’t believe how small the man looked. *What happen to all that rah-rah?* He looked like a frighten kitten about to get devoured by the gargantuan hawk.

“Lester do we got a problem here?” Bubba growled stepping towards the man.

“No-No there’s no problem. They’re kids, they just had a misunderstanding sorry to bother you Frank. C’mon boy let’s get out of here.”

Just like that the man was gone. After that incident, every time I would see him he was always nice to me. The power of fear was extraordinary and I’m not going to lie I wanted it. I’d rather be feared than to be stepped on. I didn’t know what Bubba did to get, but I wanted it.

Life never stops moving and keeping up was challenging, school was still difficult, and being outnumbered by so many white kids in your class was something I thought I would never get used to. I was definitely out of my elements. One night a new program was coming on T.V. and everybody was talking about watching Alex Haley’s Roots. I wasn’t ready for what my young eyes were about to bear witness. But there I was glued to the television set in disbelief. That night my world was shattered into a million pieces. No one had ever told me we were once slaves. I went to bed that night torn as stained tears masked my face. Sleep was impossible. How could white people be so evil? Why do they hate us so much? Why? Why? Why? A gust of anger began to seep into my soul. The protective veil was lifted. I finally saw this country for what it was and what they real thought about black people.

The very next day I went to school, I felt the cold stares and heard the silent whispers. This was the last place I wanted to be. It felt awkward and being one of two blacks in my class. It didn't help that all eyes were on us. This was the first time where I really missed Chicago. I wanted to move back home into my old world and escape the new one. I went to visit my grandmother Annette Sullivan. She was my rock my voice of reasoning and I knew I could always voice my concerns to her. She told me the naked truth. She said, "Yes we live in a cold-cold world, but that doesn't mean you have to walk around with your coat all the time." Having long talks with my grandmother were the best. She always lifted my spirits. "If them white folks go to messing with my baby I will be on the first thing smoking. I will come out there and tackle them," she laughed.

After spending Spring Break in Chicago I came back to Aurora with a new perspective, but I still was damaged, goods I couldn't shake those unpalatable vivid images out of my head. The beatings. The lynching. The hanging. The rapes. I now had distaste in my mouth for white people and I couldn't suppress it. Now I understood why black folks on the South Side of Chicago didn't trust nor like white people. No one ever told me about the true history of Black folks in America, and to watch it on TV, it was a "wow" moment. Changes, I was definitely going through it and I knew I was never going to be the same again.

TEENAGE BLUES

At the age of thirteen I was growing wild like an untamed weed. The battles I could not win, my older sister Twanda didn't have to fight for me anymore. I could handle myself. Fighting was never my forte, but like they say if you keep getting hit hard enough eventually you will learn how to hit back. No doubt I had a chip on my shoulder and over the years it had grown bigger.

We finally said goodbye to Lake Street Apartments and moved to Jefferson Court, which was further west of Aurora. A lot of my friend's families were moving also. It was like everybody was in a race to get out the slum. By this time, I was senseless to the feeling of moving, but this was what my mother did, she moved around always searching for something better.

Jefferson Court (JC) was an upgrade, we moved into a 3-bedroom town home with a full basement and 1½ bathroom. By far this was the best place we had lived as of yet. It was still a low-income residence, but the place was decent. Instead of going to Jefferson Middle School I chose to continue going to school with my friends who went to Washington Middle School. It was my responsibility to get there. I either caught the city bus or I walked. To keep money in my pockets I had a paper route in Ivy Glen Circle. I loved to hustle and putting old dead Presidents in my pockets was all I cared about. I was always thinking of ways to make money. I just hated being broke and I admit sometimes I took what others had that wasn't mine. If I had to run game to get it, I did that too. I use to walk pass big fancy houses dreaming one day that will be me trimming my hedges or mowing my yard. I hated people who laughed at me, because of the clothes or shoes I wore. My mother used to buy me cheap shoes from Kmart or Zayre. The kids would call them rabbit chasers. I wanted the Converses or the Nikes. My mother made it perfectly clear if I wanted the name brand shoes and clothing I was going to have to buy it myself.

Living in JC was a different change of pace. I found my crowd, other young teenage kids looking for something to get into. Like any other huge complex where the poor meets the poor drama will unfold. Fights were not uncommon, families fighting families, dogs fighting dogs, kids fighting kids and the parents would be the ringleaders. My fondest memories of living in JC were hanging out at the Earl's house with Kenneth, Erik and Kevin. We had some good times fishing down by the Fox River or riding our bikes on the bike path all the way to Elgin. We played tackle football in front of Sleepy's building or shooting hoops at the center by the pool. We always found something to do.

I can't forget playing Atari 2600, man they had all of the games. I never wanted to go home. Their mother Ms. Ruth use to burn in the kitchen. Every time she asked if I wanted stay for dinner the answer was always yes, yes, yes. To this day she is the main reason why I love to cook. Thank you Ms. Ruth.

JC was full of characters. How can I ever forget my dude, Bernard "Bernie Mac" Andrews, he was one of the smooth and funny kids in JC. Andrew, Brian, Lil' Amp, Quint, Andre, Charles, Tim, Tyrone, Rory, and the list goes on. J.C. reminded me of back home Chicago it was predominately black and we looked out for each other. My uncle Dennis came to live with us, and it was good seeing him. It reminded me of old times. But Dennis was still Dennis and he loved his Beer. He knew I kept a stash of money so he would try to hustle me out of some of it to get beer money. We gambled shooting Nerf hoop or playing baseball in the basement. He thought he had an easy prey but ultimately I became a worthy opponent.

What Dennis did do for me was sharpen my game and confidence when it came to sports. Sometimes I would win all his money and charge him interest to borrow it back. Looking back, I can't really complain about my early childhood years. It was a miracle to have made it out. I won some battles and I loss some battles. I fell out of trees. Rode my bike without a helmet. I jumped off rooftops. I almost drowned at camp. I stay out just before the streetlights came on. Teachers whooped me with huge wooden paddles. But hey I made it.

I tried out for the basketball team while attending Washington Middle School, and to my surprise I made it, but I was on the B team. But that was ok this was my first year playing organized basketball and I will admit I was embarrassed because my friends from Westwood (Pete, William and Marvin) played on the A team.

They were more skilled then I was, but I said to myself one day I'm going to be better than all of them. I was a beast in baseball for my age. Dennis use to pitch me grown man fastballs and I use to smack them into the field. But when my mother took me off the baseball team years ago because I cursed out the school bus driver Ms. Cobbs, I guess baseball sort of died in me. My pursuit for baseball was never strong again.

I became obsessed with the game of basketball. My favorite team was the Chicago Bulls, Reggie Theus was that dude. But my favorite player was Dr. J. I begged my stepfather Bubba to take me to a Bulls game. He agreed and on the night Philly was in town. I waited for him to come home and he never showed up. I was devastated, he later explained that him and his buddy Bill "Mavs" Foster were together hanging out, they had drugs in the car, and they were doing their thang. One thing I could always say about Bubba he always kept it one hundred. The next time Philly came to town, we had great seats and I finally got to see the game I loved up close and personal. No one had ever taken me to a sporting event and for him to do that for me that really touched my heart.

I was walking home from school one day and I saw a girl that literally almost made my heart stop beating. She was in 7th grade and I was in 8th and man she was the bomb to me. When I saw where she lived I made sure I walked passed her house everyday hoping to get a glimpse of her. Her name was Trina Milan and she was a cute pie. If she would've touched, me I would've fainted. I was at the age where my hormones were shooting through the roof. I was shy as a teen and didn't like the way I looked. Kids could be mean and some of the hurtful things they say negative about you. If your mind, don't know any better you start believing that crap. I was called ugly, nappy head, darkie. They talk about you from head to toe. So I learned to clap back and started talking about them.

I was terrified to approach her, but one day, I saw her by her locker talking to a girl named Faye. I mustered up enough courage to shoot my shot. I handed her a letter and dipped. In the letter I poured my little heart out to her in poems and corny love songs. De Barge was hot at the time so I wrote, "I like the way you comb your hair. I like the stylist clothes you wear. It's just the little things you do to show how much you really care. Ooooooooh and I like it!" Yeah I was corny and puppy love was in the air. She never gave me the time or the day, but she did read and like my corny love letters. Trina Milan, I thank you for giving me a vision of puppy love.

Hanging with the kids from Westwood I knew I had more in common with them then I did with some of the other kids from Lake Street, JC, or Heritage Green. Gang life was spreading rapidly like cancer and I found myself embroidered in the middle of it. JC was Gangster Disciple territory and so were a lot of other places I hung out at. I was friends with a lot of GDs and Vice Lords, but it was something about the Vice Lords that drew me in even further. It seemed like everybody wanted to be a gangster. It was the thing to be. In my opinion, Vice Lords were different. They were cool and much more laid back. They didn't draw off of numbers. At the age of fourteen, I became a full-fledged Imperial Insane Vice Lord member.

Some of my gangster friends didn't take to well with me being a Vice Lord. So I was involved in fights and arguments. On a hot summer night, I was hanging out in Heritage Green where I often played ball at Smith Elementary School with Hamp, Omar, JJ and Kenny Gray. I was talking to a kid named Steve Coachman who I've known from Lake Street Apartments along with his brothers Boon and Eric. Steve thought it was a good idea to call me a hook. Calling a Vice Lord, a hook was disrespectful it was like calling me a bitch.

He was locked inside of his building with his face pressed up against the glass window. He kept laughing and calling me a hook. Heated I jumped off my bike and punched him in the face through the small glass window. Glass was everywhere and Steve began jumping up and down crying hysterically. "My eye my eye," he sobbed. I could see blood pouring down his face and I didn't run when his mother Brenda came out. Steve and I have always been good friends like family and we often joke about what when on that night. But the word hook never came from his lips again.

My life changed pretty quickly when I got to West Aurora High School. I grew a couple more inches and my voice was changing. I stood just over 6 foot and I was kinda feeling myself. I still had my paper route and my dreams of being a hoop star, was still alive.

Walking through the halls of West Aurora was awesome. I heard so much about this place now I was finally seeing it for myself what high school was all about. Ever since I was in 5th grade, I listened to every game West Aurora had on the WMRO am radio. I dreamed one day the crowd would be yelling my name and the radio broadcasters would be talking about me like the Darryl Tribble or Curtis "Wolf" Pryor, or Alan Kinnebrew.

My freshmen year, yet again I was on the B team. I was always good enough to make the team but I wasn't good enough to play in the rotation with the top players. The kid from Lake Street, who dribbled the basketball all the time, Randy Norman, was a senior. He was one of my idols along with All-American Kenny Battle. Growing up watching them, become great made me want to be great. I was a student of the game and I understood the importance of playing for a program like West Aurora. Gordy Kerkman was a no non-sense coach and to play for him I was going to have to be good.

One day my friend Marvin Dean and I were coming out of class and we ran into Kenny Battle in the hallway. Marvin told him I cut all the articles of him out of the newspaper. Quite naturally I was embarrassed because that was my private domain that I let Marvin look at. But Kenny was a good sport he gave me a high five. "One day you're going to be in the NBA I know it," I told him." Kenny Battle was one of the most exciting high school basketball players in America. Every game was sold out. People came from all over to watch the show. It was pandemonium and I had a front row seat.

What I admired most about Kenny Battle was his tenacity. He gave you all he had. The brother was a joy to watch.

My high school years were flying by and I was now a junior. Initially I had not planned on trying out to play varsity basketball even though it was my dream. I had lost my way and my confidence was shot. Bottom line it was just too much good competition to compete with. But had it not been for Coach Curtis Shaw telling me I had potential I probably would've never came out. During my sophomore year I was in my art class painting a portrait of Michael Jordan. Although I had gotten better, I still wasn't good enough to make it off the bench to get some playing time. I was ready to give up my dream but coach Shaw lit a fire in me that I will forever be grateful.

The word potential gave me life it allowed me to continue my dream. My dream was to be able to become a starter and excel in the game I loved. Marvin Willis was a good friend of mine and we hung out tight. He lived on May Street along with Kenny Cahill another close friend. We were all hoopsters and we all wanted to be great. Corwin Hunt was the star of our team. He was a sharp shooter and a very good ball player. I said to myself if I could shoot half as good as him I wouldn't be sitting on the bench.

In practice, Coach Kerkman used Marvin and I as test dummies to guard Corwin. Of course Corwin took turns wearing us out. But I loved guarding him because I was learning the game from him. I took it as a challenge instead of an assignment. Corwin had that swag when he walked on the court. He knew he was the Man. And his game backed it up.

One of the things I hated about life was death. It just kept coming and you didn't know who it was going to get next. Boarding the bus getting ready to go on a road game, my friend, Bernard "Bernie Mac" Andrews was shot and killed. This was another hard pill to swallow. Life seemed so unfair and it seemed like death was always peeking around the corner.

Again my mother had us on the move. We moved from JC to Cameo Park and now we were living in Fox Croft. Fox Croft was the best neighborhood ever. I will give her credit for this; one she hit a homerun. Fox Croft was a predominately middle class white neighborhood. We had sprinkles of black families mixed in the sea and we all knew where each other lived; Michelle, Laticha, James, Nichole, Billy, Marlo, Tracey, Kendrick and Curtis.

Our lives in Fox Croft were going great until one evening there was a knock on the door. There were two uniformed Aurora Police Officers at the door. We were told to call my dad's house in Chicago they were trying to get in touch with us. Instantly my heart fell to the floor. I had a bad feeling something was going on with my grandmother. I watched in horror as my mother delivered the heartbreaking news. My grandmother Annette Ann Sullivan died of a stroke. That night I found myself aimlessly walking in the autumn fall tears flowed like a river streaming down my cheeks. My lifeline, my rock and the only person in this world who understood me, was gone. I hated life and I didn't believe God truly loved us. Because if he did, why would he allow my people to suffer? Why would he take ones we love the most? I had so many questions without answers rambling though my head. I thought it would explode.

After my grandmother was laid to rest, I fell into a deep depression. I was breathing but I wasn't living. Mostly I kept to myself. Even meeting Jeffery Osborne and Whitney Houston back stage at a concert couldn't lift me out of the funk I was in. Things would get worse before they got better. I started hanging out with my brothers down on Liberty Street, drinking beers and smoking a little pot. One night, I was riding my bike home and a pickup truck tried to run me off the road and I crashed into a field scaring up the back of my left leg. The truck slowed and the white men who were riding on back of the truck began throwing beer bottles. "Run coon boy," I heard one of them yell.

Black rage instantly filled my heart and I reached in my pocket and pulled out a silver 22 automatic and in a frantic motion I began squeezing off rounds until the gun jammed. I don't think I hit anyone, but to see them haul ass and scared out of their minds was a powerful feeling of pure elation. Had I not had that gun on me I don't know what would've happen to me.

That night when I got home I licked my wounds and I told my stepfather "Bubba" what happen. He was concerned and asked why was I carrying a gun? I told him because everybody else does, which was true. Having a gun meant you had a powerful big brother on your team that could cause fatal damage. I understood this at a young age. With Bubba I could talk about anything. He was the wisest man I knew. He was like a philosopher. He would say deep phrases that would have you thinking for days. I guess that's why I articulate myself so well when I speak. I want to leave an impression.

My mother and my stepfather's relationship started falling apart; they argued more than I could stand. One day, I was so fed up listening to them arguing I burst in their room. "If y'all can't get a long y'all don't need to be together. I'm tired of listening to this every day!" I yelled from the top of my lungs. Now mind you I was just a 16-year-old teenager. They both looked at me speechless. Bubba had pulled me to the side to talk to me on a man-to-man level. Like always he spoke with careful words. He told me anytime you have something on your mind always speak it.

I assumed they were at odds about the night before when I had to wrestle a 38 handgun away from my mother. A woman had come to our house looking to fight my mother. That was a huge mistake on the woman's part. My mother was no punk when it came to throwing' hands. She snatched the woman by her blouse and pulled her into the house and began beating her like she stole something.

My mother was so enraged that this woman had the audacity to come to our home. She went and grabbed a gun. Fast on my feet I quickly maneuvered my way towards my mother and took the gun away from her. The woman was so scared she pissed on our carpet. I swear there was never a dull moment in our household.

One Saturday morning I was walking to Colonial Café Restaurant where I worked as a busboy and dishwasher on weekends. An Aurora Police patrol car rolled up on me. Naturally I froze in fear. This was the third time the cops had stopped me, but this time they had their guns drawn. "Let me see your hands," the white cop yelled.

I did what I was told and got on the ground. After I told him I just a 16-year-old kid walking to work he determined I was good to go. Later he stated I matched the description of a burglar in the area. I knew what the real reason was, (WWB) walking while black. I was getting tired of the BS and these racial tactics. It made me even more, angrier when they made up excuses just to stop you and see who you were. My run in's and mistrust of the Police Department were just getting started. Little did I know, it was going to become a major problem.

GIRLS, GIRLS, GIRLS

My senior year was upon me and I was busting my butt working like a slave in the cotton field all summer long mowing lawns for the Aurora Township Youth Services to get money. I was always a hard worker. I would mow about 8 yards a day; big or small it didn't matter. I had been working for Jeff Scull and the Aurora Township for the last two summers. We were about to open a new Youth Center on the west side over on Gale Street. Jeff wanted me to create a new Aurora Township Youth design. They were going to put it on t-shirts and hats, and even the vehicles. I was honored to make that happen it took me two days to create and the new logo was ready for print.

I loved working with kids so working for the Township as a Junior Youth Counselor was right up my alley. It was something I was willing to pursue as a career. That summer I continued to work hard and stack my money for school. When I wasn't working I was on the basketball court practicing every chance I got. The next day I would do it all over again. I studied Michael Jordan's game like a textbook. He was the new budding rising star in the NBA. After having a long talk with Coach Kerkman at the end of my junior season, I couldn't believe he ranked me 13th going into my senior year. I was devastated so I vowed I was going to prove him wrong. I was going to be a starter on this team, he couldn't see it, but I did.

When the school year started I came back a new creation and to me the girls were looking sweet like candy and I couldn't wait to taste every flavor. My swag was different and the girls were coming at me like I was a rock star. The kid they once considered less appealing was now being slipped letters and phone numbers left and right. I couldn't wait to showcase my new skills on the basketball court. No one had seen the new me and I was ready to soar high. When it came to girls I was selective, meaning I just didn't settle for anything. After a failed relationship with a girl name Abigail, I decided to get ready for the season and the next girl would have to be special.

Christmas break had arrived and every year West Aurora High School played in the Pontiac Christmas Tournament down in Pontiac, Illinois. One thing about this team we always had a good time. When we traveled, low key, we loved the girls and we loved to party. Mad Dog 20/20 and cold beer always sounded good to us. Our season wasn't going too well we started off a miserable 0-6. All of this wasn't sitting right with me. I waited a long time for this moment and it wasn't going as planned.

However, the girls were picking and choosing and this cute chick was stalking me. She was small, petite, and wore an irresistible smile. She said I look like Ralph Tresvant from New Edition.

Later that night I snuck out the Fiesta Motel along with Kenny Cahill, he was always my partner in crime. Kenny and I have known each other ever since we met in Lake Street Apartments. I had the girls meet us down the street. I slid in the front seat of the blue 4-door Chevy Caprice and Kenny jumped in the back with a slim Puerto Rican girl. They took us back to their tiny apartment a few blocks away for a nightcap. She was 21 and I was 17. Two days later I was back home and huge snow flurries were coming down like a blizzard was approaching. The phone rings and my mother voices her displeasure about all the little girls who have been calling the house.

"Hello!" I answered.

"Hey how far is your house from The Fox Valley Mall?"

My mouth fell to the floor. This was the young woman I met in Pontiac at the basketball tournament. I couldn't believe she drove all the way to Aurora to see me. Yes, I thought she was cute, but she was a groupie and I was smart enough to know you don't make them your girl. Quickly I called (Cutch) Kenny Cahill and he came over because she had her buddy for him. All four of us hung out at Gala West in Naperville playing video games. It was late so we headed back to my house and sat in the car fogging up the windows trying to find air to breathe. I was experiencing groupie love at an all-time high and I was not complaining. After every game on the road or at home they would be waiting to get a few hugs or slide you their phone number.

One of my fondest memories of a wild groupie encounter was when we were playing on the road against Streamwood. I was minding my own business listening to some LL. Cool J on my Walkman. The sophomores were playing and we had to wait until the 3rd quarter to go back and get ready for the Varsity game. I noticed my teammates Randy, Paul, DD, kirk and David engrossed in conversation with a couple of cuties. I had to get a snicker bar before every game this was my ritual. As I turned to walk back into the gym a young smiling girl with almond joy eyes and a vibrant smile blocked me from entering the gym.

"Damn you so fine," she beamed.

"Okay thank you," I said really not knowing what to say.

We properly introduce ourselves and casually walked around the school chatting it up. We dipped in a blind spot and the next thing I knew she attacked me placing her soft lips all over mines. This girl was on fire I could feel the heat as our bodies grinded at a frantic pace. It took a minute for me to pry myself away from her stronghold. This girl was aggressive she ripped my shirt and left scratches on my back. When I made it to the locker room the team was almost fully dressed. As we were running out on the court to go through our pre-game warm-ups she leaped from the sidelines and grabbed a hold of me and would not let go. This was the most bizarre encounter I have ever had with a girl I just met. Later, Coach Kerkman asked me what do I be doing to these girls?

I shrugged, "Coach I have no idea."

The girls didn't stop coming and my play on the basketball court was getting better. I finally earned my way into the starting line-up a dream that finally came to fruition. For years I dreamed of this and to see it finally come true made me want to burst in tears of joy but I kept my composure. When Coach Kerkman, placed my name on the chalkboard as a starter, immediately Marvin Willis turned around and shook my hand and said, "Congratulations." Although I was excited I felt bad for my friend.

He was in a spot I was trying to win and we were really good friends. I rewarded coach with good play and we went on a winning streak. To finally be in the spotlight was an awesome feeling. It was like a drug that you can't describe, but you knew you needed it. I worked my ass off against all odds battling the coach on and off the court. Sometimes he would yell at me until he was blue in the face. "You're not Michael Jordan," he would scream. Looking back what I really admired about Coach Kerkman is he was teaching us how to respect the game the right way. When you're a 17-year old kid you think you know everything and coach had no problem with knocking you down off your high horse. I thank him for teaching us how to transition from boys to young men. It was a turning point in my life how I dressed and how I conducted myself as a respectable young man. West Aurora High School and Coach Kerkman was good to me; I will be forever grateful.

My basketball life was going great and my love life was up next. Her name was Nichole Stewart. She was a blessing. She was young, beautiful, and had a smile that stole my breath. We quickly started dating and eventually she became my girlfriend. Other girls who were pursuing me were not happy. They couldn't understand what I saw in a freshman. What Nichole had, none of them could hold a candle to her. She was mature, very nurturing, and I was in love with her. No other girl could make me feel like that. I loved her family even her dogs Ruffer and Garfield. Her beautiful mother was a sweetheart; no matter what, she was always kind to me. Even when Nichole and I were no longer together, we still kept in contact.

ON MY OWN

My high school days were over and I felt like Patti Labelle, *on my own.* College was up next for me and I had several offers to attend out of states schools. But I decided to stay close to home and play for Waubonsee College. Waubonsee College was located in Sugar Grove, Illinois about 7 miles outside of Aurora. It was a small division III school and they were trying to turn it into a powerhouse. I didn't know too much about Waubonsee but I did know a guy named Kevin Avery was a star there and now he was in Nebraska. Dave Heiss was the head coach and I knew of him because he once played in the West Aurora program.

I had a very successful freshman year of college I averaged 17.2 and I couldn't do nothing more but get better. Basketball was beginning to come easy for me and I was blossoming into something special. After I dropped 30 on Morton Grove other colleges started contacting me. My relationship with Coach Heiss became estranged. We bumped heads on many occasions. I felt he was a good player coach but he wasn't a good head coach. Our team was short on players and talent. Off the court coach was cooler than a fan. On the court you were every name in the book and I didn't sign up for that part of the game. You can't treat your players like dirt then expect them to perform for you.

I was emotionally spent and my patience was wearing thin. My grades started to slip and I was tired of eating eggs sausages sandwiches and chips out of the vending machines. I was on my own and I was dead broke. I did odd end jobs on the weekend when I could to keep money in my pockets. I had a car that always broke down and every dime I got I poured it into that sucker. So after a year and a half I dropped out of college. A year ago I had broken off my relationship with my girl for no other reason than I was being an jackass. The coach for Lewis University had contacted me and they were willing to deal with me. But I was so frustrated without having any money in my pockets I had to go get a job. Basketball was on hold until I could figure things out.

Me and the homie, Kenny Cahill was hanging out one night riding around listening to some house music. We were House Heads and Kenny was an aspiring DJ. Most of our weekends consisted of riding out to Elgin or Chicago always looking for something to get into. However, this weekend we were hanging out at Aurora College where Mike" Hitman" Wilson and Maurice "Ice" Culpepper use to DJ before they became famous. We were there enjoying a party they often threw on the weekends and that's when a girl named Minnie Mae caught my eye. I knew of her because years ago her and my older sister had gotten into a fight.

She stood about 5 feet 5 inches, cute in the face and slim in the waist. For some reason, I couldn't take my eyes off her. I had seen her many times, but tonight I saw something else.

It didn't take long for us to become an item. In the fall of 88 we began dating. At the time she was staying in Eastwood, next door to the future R&B Bad Boy star Carl Thomas. Eastwood was the hood and it was well known as Gangster Disciples territory. That alone was going to become a problem. There were a lot of gangsters I grew up with and we were like family. The Stewart family was one of them. They had a huge family one of the biggest in Aurora down to the southern state of Mississippi. In the 80's and 90's Eastwood was considered a dangerous high crime area. But I loved it. I had some of the best times there. It was home.

I was working full time in West Chicago on 3rd shift with the homey Toby Dunn. I was in the real world unsure of what direction I was heading in. Toby and I had visions of making it in the rap game. We started cutting demos and doing talents shows all over the Chicago land area. Toby was a talented lyricist and I thought we could have a shot. However, I knew working was a must because without your own income you couldn't survive. For the first time in my life I was missing basketball and I felt like a lost sick puppy who couldn't find his way home. The inner voice of reasoning was telling me to go back to school. Not listening to that inner voice would cost me dearly.

Minnie had two small girls named Sherece and Sharon. I knew if I continued to see her I was going to have to accept her children as well. I was 19 years old and I knew nothing about raising kids. I was at a crossroad because a lot of people didn't approve of me dating her. She had a wild reputation but I found that to be intriguing. I saw a diamond in the rough waiting to shine. She was smart, attractive and she had some hustle about herself.

She too had a huge family totaling 8 other siblings and a host of nieces and nephews. Her mother Luevinia was a God fearing woman who I loved. No matter if I was wrong or right she always had my back and that was all love.

Quickly I was thrust into the role of a provider. We had our own apartment and at times things could get overwhelming. I wanted more for the 4 of us and I felt like I was on an island by myself. I wanted the good life and to escape the of land poverty. The dead end jobs weren't paying enough for me to be able to raise a family. I competed for some of the best jobs and got turned down job after job. Some of them only required a high school diploma and I noticed white people were getting jobs with no problem. I knew wearing this black skin was the cause of it. Some of the employers would look you up and down and as soon as you left, your application would be tossed in a garbage can.

I had a family and as a man I felt it was my duty to produce and be a provider. To make some extra money I caved in to the temptations and began selling powder cocaine. Never in a million years had I thought I would be selling drugs. But in my mind this was not going to be a career it was just going to be for a hot minute and I'm out. I always kept a job and selling drugs became a part time job. I didn't really know the ends and out of the dope game but I was learning on the fly.

At this time in my life, life was bittersweet. Death claimed three people who I had mad love for. My brothers Aaron and Morris died of gun violence and one of homey's mother died in her sleep. I never did like going to funerals because I didn't want to see their lifeless body lying cold in a box as if they were sleeping. I didn't want that image of them etched in my memory of them. I understand we all have to die, but damn death seemed so cold you could be here today and gone tomorrow.

I had other issues to worry about; my stepfather "Bubba" was falling off the map. He was very sick and he looked it. However, I was fearing the worse and hoping for the best. But his condition was deteriorating fast. Although he and my mother were no longer together she still cared for him. These were tough times and I just couldn't turn a blind eye. I was driving my new car passing through downtown headed to the Westside. I saw him go into Wayside Mission on Lincoln and New York Street. He looked so small and feeble it hurt my heart to see him like that. Because at one time Bubba was a big man standing a solid 6'3 225, I pulled over, parked, and wept. I couldn't stop the tears from falling. There were rumors of him having AIDS through drug use. I was starting to believe them; even though he told me himself they were untrue. I knew he used heroin and I witnessed it get the best of him. I was now in the streets so I knew people who knew things.

I stood outside and waited for him. When he came out I handed him five hundred dollars and told him I loved him. As a family we didn't toss the words I love you around much. For reasons I don't know why I could see his eyes turning misty. It really hurt him to take it, but he knew he needed it. He praised me on becoming a fine young man and he dropped a jewel of wisdom on me. "Never let your demons get the best of you," he said. Unfortunately, that was the last time I saw him 3 months later he died. I promised him in death I would always look after my little brother and keep him out of harm's way.

Death was not a friend of mines because it always takes the ones you love. It was heartbreaking to lose the man who put up an effort to be a father to me when my biological father hadn't shown up yet. I know my stepfather had his demons but overall he was good to us and I learned so much from him in such little time. God bless his soul.

In the fall of '91 God sent me a gift, my son Kwmane Octravious O'Keith Harris was born. I couldn't believe it, I had a son. The joy I felt was overwhelming. A little me who looked just like me. That was a wow moment and for months I carried that boy with me everywhere I went. With me having a son I knew I had to make a better life for him even if it meant I had to sacrifice my own. I wanted to give him everything I didn't have. I wanted him to have the best of everything. *People will not be laughing and talking about the clothes he wore.*

When the crack rock epidemic hit in the town in early 90's the town was lit. Fiends were no longer looking for the powder packs they were looking for ready rocks. The movie New Jack City hit and everybody wanted to be Nino Brown or Scarface's Tony Montana. We finally saw away out the hood where we could be able to feed our families. We didn't realize at the same time we were destroying our own hoods and communities.

The dope game was on and poppin'. It was like milk and honey was everywhere, everybody could eat. I went from eight balls to quarter keys in a hurry. Money was good and when I held my first $30,000 I thought I was rich you couldn't tell me nothing. I was so paranoid I had to watch everybody. I didn't tell a soul how much money I was making. You just couldn't trust anyone not even the ones you loved. Everybody wanted something: family, friends, enemies, police and everybody and their mama. I used to unscrew the vents in the walls to hide my money in the walls.

No matter where I went all eyes were on me. I was in the spotlight all over again but this time I was not playing basketball. Life was good and money was being made hand over fist. The Chicago Bulls were winning NBA Championships, what more could you ask for? But like saying goes, the more money you make the more problems you have. In a blink of an eye my world started crumbling and slowly I started spiraling out of control. Cats I had working for me kept having their money coming up short. So I had two choices, one I could take my loss and move on or two I could keep throwing money into the gutter and watch it disappear. I chose to move on and keep my foot on the petal.

When people see you winning some of them won't be clapping for you. I was hearing rumors that some folks were plotting to rob me and the cops were going to be kicking in my front door. Of course this was a concern I always had because when you're in the dope game you become a hot boy. Everything I did I saw people watching me. Fearing for the worst, I kept a gun with me or near me. I stopped working a regular job and that's something I never did. But I was stuck in the game and I was trying to win. I had too many people depending on me so I had to find a way to win. All my life I knew I was destined to be somebody. I just had to find my own lane to drive in.

Against all odds I was in it to win it. But the rabbit foot wasn't on my side anymore. I was at a house on the eastside cooking up 2 ounces of cocaine when the police were outside banging on the door demanding entrance. Quickly, I broke up the dope and flushed it down the toilet. After the cops couldn't find what they were looking for in so many words they told me they were on to me. After that close encounter, I kept taking L's. I couldn't win for losing. I went to a party to meet a Mexican connect that had some major weight on Peruvian flakes. Peruvian flakes were like the best dope in town, meaning it hasn't been stepped on 4 or 5 times. The fiends loved it. To be in this room was big time and cocaine was everywhere. Freestyle music was blasting from a DJ in the back of the room.

People were dancing and taking turns snorting cocaine off of a large square mirror.

I was definitely out of my elements. I felt like a deer in headlights and the Mexican Inka could smell it. “You don’t want no pica?” he asked Pointing towards the pile of cocaine on the mirror.

I kindly declined and he then whispered into the ear of the Latino brother I came with.

“Aye Cool, man you don’t wanna do no white lines?”

I looked at the Latino brother like he had lost his mind. “Man I don’t get down with no coke.”

“Man he thinks you might be a nard bro. So if you don’t party he won’t deal with you.”

So there I was stuck in a predicament. If I could go back in time, I definitely would have walked my ass right on out of there and never looked back. But I let the little voice on my shoulder win. I took a couple of bumps of cocaine from off the mirror and my nose burned like hell. The man watched me closely and he smiles. After the burning sensation went away, I felt a nice drain run down my nose and wow, now I could see why people loved this drug so much. It was like a cosmic rush.

I tossed back a couple cold bottles of Budweiser and took in the atmosphere. Girls were partying and shoving free coke up their nose like it was candy. So this was the life. I remember telling myself walking out of there with the most Cocaine I ever had, stuffed in my briefs. *Damn! What the hell did I get myself into?*

MY TRUTHS

I *am grateful for my Mother's teachings blessed to still be breathing.*

Born in a world where the devil seeks to defeat you. The dirt of Chicago birthed me

We didn't have much, but my Mother's touch and to be truthful sometimes that wasn't enough.

Pop's wasn't there so I didn't care had to find his love from the streets who, was always there.

Being broke as a joke wasn't No joke.

I didn't see, nothing funny about wearing a cheap coat.

The Windy City hawk was cold and you had to be strong to withstand its chokehold.

The cold got colder with every step I took.

The older I got it looks like I was going to be a crook.

From childlike eyes I was wise beyond my years

I saw the world for what it is.

Drenched in poverty set of the stagecoach for arm robberies.

The hate is real when the system is set up to kill.

People will size you up in three seconds spit you out in four

Now that's real.

Don't tell me the sky is falling when I know the truth.

I am who I am, but one thing I know is my truths.

GROWING PAINS

They say if you play the game long enough, be prepared to suffer a few setbacks. Setbacks were an understatement and my habit for the drug of cocaine began to breathe. The new drug of choice was called macking where we take weed and sprinkle crack cocaine on it. Damn, near everybody and their momma were doing this drug. I felt like Henry Hill from Good Fellas. I was running around like a chicken with its head cut off.

It seemed like every other week I was fighting and going to jail. A lot of people with a habit won't admit they have one. I was no different. My relationship with my son's mother started deteriorating and she started distancing herself doing her own thing. It was like ever since she had my son she wanted to run wild in the wind. This woman was very smart and I always tried to bring the best out of her. I felt she loved controversy and drama more than she loved me. Everything seemed to be closing in on me. I couldn't trust anyone and that was a lonely feeling. At times I felt like I was on an Island all by myself. The demons were hashing flames and I could feel the slow burn.

I had just come home from working all day and my son's mother's nephew Pimp was with me. The sun was still out blazing the cloudless blue skies and people were out enjoying themselves. Eastwood was home, you either fit in or you stayed out of the way.

On this particular day, once again I found myself being sucked into some drama. As I was driving up Grove Street, Jermaine Stewart had flagged me down and told me about what went down with my BM (baby mama). Apparently she had gotten into an altercation with a guy from Chicago. He put his hands on her and my 2 year old son got knocked down. When another man puts his hands on your woman you would be less than a man if you didn't show up and show out.

With a strong adrenaline rush pulsating through my blood stream I quickly mashed down on the accelerator and shot back in the hole. The hole was a dead end circle on Northeast Drive where nothing good ever happened. As soon as I got out of my car, I saw a guy named Mook. Mook was a good ole country Mississippi boy. He stood tall and strong as an ox and when he opened his mouth he spoke in a low even keel tone. If anything went down in Eastwood, he would know.

"Mook, what happened?" I inquired as I approached him.

He stood up and looked me dead in my eye. "Get that nigga," he said dryly.

With sweat poppin' off my forehead, I went banging on Christie's door where I knew the guy was. In my mind I was thinking I should've grabbed one of my guns just in case he had one. I was taking a chance running up on someone I really did not know.

When the door opened, Christie tried swapping me away as though I were a fly. But she knew how I got down. It was going to be some fireworks and she just didn't want them poppin' off at her house.

I waited for him to come out. I remember thinking *why is he taking so long?* He finally came out trying to explain what happened, but I wasn't trying to buy what he was selling. A large crowd emerged suddenly out of nowhere. It didn't surprise me, because the hood loved drama. It gives them something to talk about. I picked up a huge brick and ran towards him ready to do damage. The tall slender man cowered in fear with hands over his head. I didn't want to kill him, so I tossed the brick and took my fist and hit him with a hard 2 piece and a biscuit. The man fell down to one knee. His short dark processed hair was all over his face. He recovered quickly and as he stood I noticed a sharp butcher knife fell out his blue sweat pants.

Like a scene played out of a scary movie, dude looked like a creature feature as his face contorted into an angry scowl. The mad man began chasing me around my car. Seconds later, all you heard were sirens. Police cars were pouring into the hole like a scene in a movie. Of course, the coward ran into the house and put up the knife. The police came over and began explaining to me they had taken care of the situation. I was not a happy camper and I shared my displeasure in so many choice words.

The crowd of onlookers had thicken, and while I'm still arguing with police this fool came out in front of the police looking to get some get back.

"Wasssup now?" he yelled, coming towards me.

I couldn't believe this fool was trying to fight me in front of the police. Then out of nowhere my oldest sister's boyfriend Cee Cee came from the blind side and rocked this fool with a hard right gut shot. He aimlessly staggered wildly like a drunken man and I wasted no time pushing my way passed the police. We were on him like two wild Rottweilers tearing him from limb from limb. I had on steel toe boots and I was out of my mind filled with rage that this clown had the audacity to put his hands on my woman. I used his face as a stomping ground like I was trying to put out a campfire.

The police saw this ass whopping was getting out of hand, truth-be-told had they not pulled us off of him, we probably would have killed him. Officer Shereen whom I known as a kid from Lake Street Apartments had slap the cuffs on me. I always had love for Shereen and I considered her as a friend. Besides I did cut her hair a few times. This wasn't going to be the first time she placed me under arrest and the path I was on I had a few more arrest in me.

I motioned for my sister Twanda to grab the wad of cash out of my pocket because when I was arrested before; my money came up short when I got it back. As they were stuffing me in the paddy wagon amongst the sea of the crowd I saw my girl's mother Miss V. Wheeler giving it to the police. I slightly chuckled because one thing about this woman she always had my back right or wrong.

After sitting in jail overnight on trumped up charges the judge was not pleased with the Aurora Police for bogusly holding us in jail on felony charges when actually they were only misdemeanors charges. I bonded myself, and Cee Cee out and had to pay extra for him because he had a warrant. When I returned home there were all sorts of threats flying around about what the folks were going to do to me for beating down one of their own. I took threats seriously and I stocked piled up on guns. If they wanted to go to war, I was ready.

They say what goes up must come down. Sometimes you have to learn life the hard way. My relationship with my kids' mother was going down the drain. I loved her dearly but I knew it was too toxic for me to withstand. I just didn't know how to walk away. The house was on fire and I wanted to save everyone, but seemingly I couldn't save myself. Maybe if I would've tried a little harder, being a better man, a better father, maybe things would've been different. But you can't force someone to stay when they already have one foot out the door.

CLOUDY DAYS

Everything in my life that was good was now taken. I had no one to blame but myself. The devil was talking and the sad thing was, I was listening. After several failed attempts of trying to keep my family together, it was finally over. She had moved on and I was still stuck waddling in the mud. I couldn't blame her maybe it was for the best. Nevertheless, I was crushed and the pain wasn't going anywhere no time soon.

I had moved back home with my mother and little brother. This was a low moment in my life. I suffered from depression and didn't know it. One thing about black people, when we are going through hard times, we don't seek any medical or professional help. We just deal with pain hoping somehow it will miraculously dissipate by itself.

The summer of '95 was a horrible summer. Gang bangin' was at an all-time high. A race war was going on and the Latin Kings were killing blacks like it was a sport. It was a sad time for the city especially when they killed Norman and Bam. I was benumbed to everything around me and my heart was turning colder than ice. I had seen so many people I knew in my 25 years on this earth die of a horrible death. It's a shame young black men have to carry a gun to protect themselves from their own race and other races too. Sometimes it didn't matter if you were in a gang or not, if you were young and black they automatically assumed you were a thug or a criminal. Bubba told me once never kill a man if you don't have to. The way bullets were flying around no one was safe.

Aurora made national news as Inside Edition made its way to the town. Jeff Scull from the Aurora Township contacted me about doing an interview. I declined because I didn't want to become a target for telling the truth. Months later, just when I thought my world couldn't get any worse, it did. One Sunday afternoon, the guys and I were playing football at Mc Cleerly School. Something we did often as we could.

Afterward, we headed back to our house on Lancaster and chilled out. A couple of white girls came by and one of them was talking about performing oral sex. I left for a couple of hours when I returned the girl was in the house willingly knocking guys down one by one in the bathroom. So against my better judgment, I went into the bathroom to get me one. But when I saw she had semen on her face and hands, I changed my mind.

After everyone had left the cops showed up and said a girl was gang raped, *Gang raped*? I couldn't believe what I was hearing this had to be some sort of mistake. Nothing like that ever happened. I was boiling in rage. Two days later, I made my way to the Kane County Jail. I was so sick I couldn't eat. I couldn't sleep. I was in jail for something I didn't do. On top of that the media ran the story on the front page. White girl gets gang raped. *Wow*!

The old Kane County Jail was located on Fabyan Parkway in Geneva. This was my third time visiting this place, and I hated it. Being locked in a cage like an animal was definitely inhumane. The last time I was here, I sold a D.E.A. agent an ounce of baking soda and I had gotten probation on that case, but I couldn't go down for a sex case that's not who I was and neither were the other guys who were arrested. I was determined to fight these false charges to the end.

Jail was jail and you had to find a way to survive. I was in cell - block 163. This was considered a Vice Lord cellblock. We stood 25 strong. I quickly rose to elite status and became chief enforcer of the cellblock. Hey I was in Rome and I was doing what the Romans do. My job consisted of keeping order in the house. If you weren't all mighty, you had to be respectable. If not chances were, your stay would be unpleasant. One thing about me, I never abused the power I had. I believed in peace over violence. I believed in unity over division. I liked to get along with everyone. It didn't matter if you were an opposition or neutron. Unfortunately, everyone doesn't want what you want and trouble is always lurking around the corner. If someone had beef with someone they took it to the shower area and I would let them fight one on one with security on the door. In my book, you were not a Vice Lord if you didn't know your (Lit). You can't be a part of something if you don't know anything about it.

Finally, I made bond and I fought my case for two years on the outside. In the fall of '97 I went to trial and was found not guilty. I was relieved the judge found the truth and knew the girl was lying. But to go through that humiliation was something I wouldn't wish on my worst enemy. The state of Illinois knew she was lying but still tried to send innocent young black men to prison for a crime they did not commit. I was crushed watching how dirty the system got down and a part of me wanted to seek revenge. I had people in my ear telling me let God handle it. *Watch, she is going to get what she got coming.* I believe in God, but at the time I wasn't trying to hear that. This lying chick is the one who needed to be in jail. My lawyer told me I could sue her, but for what, she didn't have anything.

After clearing my name, I was hoping to get back to being me. But the drugs and alcohol didn't want to let go of me. No matter how hard I tried to break free at times my brain felt like it was being high jacked at gunpoint. I hated myself for being so weak when I knew I had a giant living inside me that could overcome any adversity. During these cloudy days in my life, I still managed to somehow spend time with the kids. My son even lived with me a time or two. However, I did battle homelessness and sleeping in my car and seedy places. A lot of people would be embarrassed to talk about their painful past. But I don't feel that way. I believe everyone has a story that can help someone. We as people must uplift instead of tearing down. Cloudy days do not discriminate. We all must walk through the storms.

In the spring of '98, I started working for a moving company in Du Page County. At times, this job brought a glimmer of hope back into my life. The owner was a white man who had a substance abuse problem. That's how I met him. One cold winter night, I was stacked up in an auto mechanic shop and this white dude walks in wearing surf pants. Of course, he reminded me of a plant that might be wearing a wire so he wasn't going to get served because I did not trust him. However, he did tell me he owned a moving Company and gave me a card. A few months later I contacted him and began working for his company. He gave me a chance to prove myself something I was use to by being the black guy.

Every day I felt like I had to always prove myself not only to white folks, but also to my own people. I was learning being black you had to work a lot harder than anyone else. I have always been a hard worker and working in the moving business was hard labor. But I had the mentality of a lion. If you show me the money, you would hear my roar, because I was coming for it.

The moving game was like any other game. It was a hustle and I learned to work it with ease. I was young, fit and strong and I could out work two men with ease. I hustled my way up to the top of the small company, at times running the business, while the owner sat at home and battling his demons. With me running the show everything was running smoothly. The customers were happy and money was being made. When I first started working for the company; the trucks they had were horrible. A couple of them needed to be in the junkyard. The owner and I formed an alliance, but at times it became indifferent. He was the type of guy who would use you up and throw you away when he didn't need you anymore. He played on your circumstances and like a doctor he loved to get inside of your head.

Once he fully taught me the game I roamed the entire United States driving from coast to coast without a valid driver's license. I knew I had an angel looking over my shoulder because I made it back safely every time. Yeah I was crazy, but I was a high-risk taker and I wasn't afraid to fail. I think that's the reason why he and I clicked so much. We both had that no hold bars compatible spirit. As I look back on it today, even though this guy turned out to be a jackass, I might not have always agreed with him, unlike others I never hated him. In a way, I felt sorry for him because I saw the hole that was buried in his heart. He kept me around for comfort and for protection, he knew I could be dangerous if I had to be and I think that kind of excited him.

The moving business had to take a back seat for a minute because I had a serious matter riding in the front seat to tend to. The Aurora Police had a warrant out for my arrest for a theft that I allegedly committed. This was a bogus charge but hey they were out to get me. For years the law had tried to sting me on drug sales sending informants and nards. But somehow I was always able to stay two steps ahead of them. They did everything in their power to destroy me. My Lawyer, Fred Morelli told me they did not like me. I couldn't understand why? However when they took my Mother's house because of me that was the straw that broke the camel's back. I was already banned from all Aurora Housing Properties now they banned me from my old neighborhood street. One thing about me, I had an uncanny nature. If you did something to me; I was going to come for you no matter who you were.

I went to court one day and I saw a childhood friend Richard Irvin. He was now a prosecutor for the State. I wasn't mad at him like so many other people who were. I was proud of him because he came where I came from and to see him make it, it was all love. When I was first arraigned on these charges, Richard was the prosecutor, and now I was back in the same courtroom. I was late getting to court to try to get the warrant squashed. But Judge Peterson, a man I didn't too much care for, denied my motion and locked me up without bail. Here I was trying to do the right thing and I get bit in the ass. I couldn't believe it *"No bond" are you freakin' kidding me*? I got four grand in my pocket and I can't get a bond on a three-hundred-dollar bail. "Wow!"

The bailiff cuffed me and led me to the holding cells down below the basement of the courthouse. I saw a guy who was a coward that had jumped me with five others. We made eye contact and as I passed by him I spit on the glass window and told him what I thought about him. I was already hotter than fish grease and I was ready to smash anything in my path. I wished they would've put me in the cell with him. The bailiff stashed me away in a small room in the corner by myself waiting for transport.

Jail was for losers and there I was back in Losersville feeling worthless. With everything going wrong in my life I was at my wits' end. I was feeling like 2Pac *F' the world.* When we got back to the jailhouse, I went through the intake process where they asked you a bunch of questions; Name? Address? Workplace? Are you suicidal? Etc.

After that they strip you down and look up your butt hole to make sure you're not bringing in any contraband or weapons. This is a job I could never do putting humans in chains and shackles, and locking them up like caged animals. To me it's a form of slavery all over again. Some people get off on having a certain amount of power over someone else. I went to school with a lot of law enforcement officers and most of them were nobody's in school. Now they got a badge and they're tough guys. I use to tell them you don't have to have a badge to shoot a gun. And just because you got a badge doesn't mean you can't be shot by a gun.

The older I got the more I began to see the world for what it was. The Man wanted money anyway he could get it. Jail was his new gold mine. After I took my shower, I was placed in a drunk tank. The drunk tank was a small concreted room where offenders were stored waiting to be housed. They kept the room cold like an icebox. Once they called your name, you grab your mattress and toiletries and head upstairs to your assigned cellblock. If you were a known trouble maker, they would purposely place you in harm's way to get your butt kicked. On this day, I had said some slick choice words that the short red head officer didn't like.

"Harris you stay back," he said.

"Stay back for what!" I replied raising my voice.

"Because I said so, now get back in that tank."

I get what he was doing. This was pay back because he felt I disrespected him and had everyone laughing at him now he wanted to flex his power. "Get me a white shirt," I spat refusing to go back into the icebox.

"Are you refusing?"

"Hell yeah! Get me a white shirt!" I screamed in his face.

That really pissed him off as his face went from pink to bright red. He shoved me toward the room. I laughed at him. "That's all you got Woody Woodpecker."

He shoved me again this time with all his force knocking one of my sandals off of my feet. This guy must have not had gotten the memo about me. I fight cops too. I shoved him back and that's when all hell broke loose. He grabbed my arm and tried to spin me around and put me in a chokehold. I used his momentum against him and flipped him on his back. The little man was scared out of his mind as I began choking him out. Seconds later, I heard keys jingling and walkie-talkie's crackling. The boys in blue had come to his rescue. After they beat my ass, they hog tied me and dragged me off to segregation.

Segregation aka SEG was called the hole. It's supposed to be this dark gloomy place where they put offenders who disobey the rules. During my short stay in jail hotel, hotel I called it. The hotel was a place where you could think, but time seemed to stand still. One day felt like 48 hours. The living conditions were not good. They gave you a thin mattress and a wool blanket. You were allowed a shower once a week, 3 meals a day and a bible. The food in segregation was less than you would receive in general population. I guess this tactic was to defer offenders from acting out. When you're deprogramed they will do anything in their power to reprogram you. I hated jail and everything it stood for. So every time I came here I felt like a loser. Deep down I knew I didn't belong here. I just couldn't grab a hold of my life and steer the ship straight.

Some of the CO's I went to school with they used to see me as a star ball player. Now I was a jailbird. As I sat in segregation battered and bruised, I began to write on anything I could get my hands on. A fire of anger and frustration was burning deep inside of me. I wrote poems. I wrote deep thoughts about my circumstances, about my life, about my pain and about my desires. *A black man deserves to be happy and free. I just wish the world could see.*

It felt really good to release my penned up emotions and as I saw my pain spill out on paper the storm began to calm. I was at peace for the moment. I enjoyed how that appeasing calm made me feel. I just wished it could last forever. The pen was nice and he spoke what he felt, no filter.

THE BIG HOUSE (PENN STATE)

A man that's lost must find his own way or he will be lost forever.

On a gloomy Tuesday morning, we were shackled up in chains and cuffs headed to the Big House (Joliet Correctional Prison.) To say I wasn't nervous would be incorrect. My eyes were wide open like a deer in headlights. For years I had heard wild stories about Joliet. I had driven passed this place many time but I never imagined I would become a prisoner there. But here I was standing in the mist of the original concrete jungle. The huge monstrous steel gate looked like something out of medieval times.

We were greeted by an old black officer he gave us the ins and outs of what to do and not to do, "If you go into a cell and there is a candy bar on the top bunk. I will advise you not to eat it. I have taken a lot of men to the hospital because they were sexually assaulted. If this is your first time to the penitentiary make it your last time. If you been here before than you are a damn fool to come back," he boldly stated.

I knew my stay in the Big House wasn't going to be long. There was a chance I could dress in and dress out. I only had a year to do. From my understanding, 61 days would be the most I would do if it came down to it. Once inside we were all ushered into an intake facility and I was branded with an IDOC number. Once you have this number you're marked for life you will always remember this number. After being poked and probed like cattle, we were all ushered to a building that was referred to as the car wash.

The car wash was a small old brick building where prisoners take showers. I can see why they call it the car wash. It was at least 100 of us lined up waiting for a wash. We were handed a cheap bar of soap and a towel. Fifteen at a time stripped down and showered. We had 2 minutes. *Welcome to the car wash.*

Everywhere we walked watchmen from the castle like towers had a rifle pointed on us. I call them watchmen because that's what they did. They watched you like a hawk. No matter how many prison movies I watched it could never compare to what I was actually witnessing. I was in the belly of the beast and this was nothing to brag about. But for some strange reason people do. We were housed in the east house and they didn't assign you to a cell. You had to find your own cell. So there I was walking up and down the gallery with a piss stained, thin mattress cradled in my arms. My hawk like face wore a hard expression letting the vultures that stood in front of their cell doors know I was not an easy mark. I was ready do battle if necessary. The first question they asked was "what mob did you belong to?" Without hesitation I blurted out, "Vice Lord."

I was finding out early that the prisoners ran the jail. So if you were gang affiliated you were housed with your mob. My first cellmate was a Traveler (VL) from the West Side of Chicago. He was a few years younger than me, short and stocky with a dark hue skin tone. Everything was funny to him. This was his third merry-go-round in the joint. This time he had to do a 5- piece dinner. A 5-piece dinner meant he had been sentenced to 5 years. He had to kick out 2 ½ years at 50 %. He claimed he had a pistol case. One thing I learned about being locked up you couldn't believe everything you heard. Men lie easily to make themselves larger than life. In prison everybody had a story, but everybody didn't always tell the truth. So you had to choose what to believe.

Everything came with a price, if you wanted to smoke you needed money. If you wanted drugs, that too came with a price. When you were in classification the only thing you were allowed to have in your possession were write outs. Write outs were stamp envelopes, and the most you could have were twenty. They were a gold mine, because all day gallery workers would be selling rolls for write outs or anything else they could tax you on. See in the county jails you couldn't smoke, but here you could smoke like a broke stove. One Write out would get you 4 thin cigarette rolls. White boys would do anything to smoke their fears away. They were badly outnumbered by the black prisoners. When the chow lined rolled all the neutrons had to fall in line. Neutrons were guys who were non-affiliated with a gang. If they broke the Vice Lord line or the Folks line, they got dealt with real quick.

Walking to the chow hall was something I dreaded because you never knew what was going to pop off. I saw a stabbing my first week and they put us on lockdown for a week. When you enter the chow hall you immediately pay attention to the watchmen who had their rifles cocked and loaded from a high position above. In the ceiling were gunshot holes from shootings that had occurred. I was sitting at a table with an old white guy and he was literary shaking like a leaf in the wind. Everybody was on alert, especially the gang members. One of my brothers had offered me a weapon, but I told him I didn't need it, because in the back of my mind I only had 61 days to serve. I was not trying to kill someone and get 61 years. I was a short timer and I was going to do my earnest to keep it that way.

Joliet Prison was not a pleasant place and I hated every minute of it. I can easily see why a man would lose their insanity. Being locked in a cage like an animal was not living and in my mind God didn't make me an animal. Nights seemed like long days and long days seemed like long nights. The living conditions were cruel and inhumane. It takes a strong man with a strong mind to be able endure this dark world. I just hoped I was one of them. For 3 weeks, I watched people come and go out of classification. I had met 7 cellmates and I was still stuck in limbo waiting to see what prison I was going to be transferred to. So there I was lying on my bunk listening to all these unknown voices, some talking, some laughing. It was a mad house. *A hotel of hell.* The only time you could think was when everybody was sleeping in the middle of the night. Then first thing in the morning a guard would come by with a steel rod running it across the bars on each cage making this god awful noise that drove you half crazy. They did this to make sure prisoners were not sawing the bars trying to escape. I had enough of Joliet. I was ready to go.

Prison was not for me. I don't know why people like to choose this life? It was like being buried alive. You couldn't touch the world, but you knew it was there. There was nothing you could do about the outside world, or about the life you once lived. Once you're locked up everything stops and your dreams and goals are put up on the shelf too. That woman you had now she's with somebody else.

If you're lucky, your family and true friends will be your best support team. I saw a lot of prisoners that weren't so lucky. They were on their own. To me the Big House was nothing more than a gateway to hell. Souls were lost and men didn't know how to be men. The frantic prison experience was horrifying. They put you in 6x10 cement cave 24 Hour lockdown, one shower every seven days, and they treat you like scum. The meals are something I wouldn't feed a dog. You had nothing to read but what was in your mind. Then you had a cellmate who you did not know nor could trust. You didn't know if he was a stone cold murderer or a sex predator. At all times you had to have your guard up because you could be harmed or killed at any giving moment.

One of my earliest disturbing disappointing memories was when I saw a young black teen being beaten by two white correctional officers. I was appalled by this barbaric behavior especially because the teen was handcuffed. I mean they beat the hell out of this poor kid. They smiled and laughed when it was over. Two days later that same young man was found hanging in his cell. Rumors has it his baby momma had ended their relationship and she began dating his cousin. My heart went out to that kid as I watched the coroner wheel his dead body down the gallery in a long black zip bag.

I was learning in a crash course that the outside world didn't matter and if you wanted to survive in the belly of the beast, you had to disconnect your emotions from it as well or else you too could find yourself being carried out in a body bag. The very next day, I woke up to a paper bag being dropped in front of my door. This was a disquieted moment that every prisoner held their breath, because inside that bag was your classification information of what facility they decide to send you to. It was a joyous moment for some because they were being sent to a sweet location and now they could get settled in and do, their time. When I heard the word sweet I was baffled because no matter where they send me there was nothing sweet about being locked up. Some of the men were disappointed about where they were going Menard, Statesville, and Vandalia were the least favored. I found out I was going to Illinois River down in Canton, Illinois. Finally, I could leave this hellhole and say goodbye to bugs, rodents, and the madness. This was one hell of an experience and I hoped to never return.

On the blue bird bus the next day, I was shackled and chained to a prisoner I did not know. We were all given a lunch bag and told to shut up. There will be no talking. If you had to use the bathroom they had a white bucket in the back. Once the bus pulled outside of the Big House, a cool sense of relief swept over me. Freedom wasn't too far away. I can now see it. I sat next to the window and gazed out at a world I was no longer a part of. As the blazing sun touched my face, I smiled for the first time in a long time and it felt good.

OUT ON THE BRICKS

After serving my remaining sentence at Illinois River Correctional Center, I said goodbye to a good Latino brother I met from Joliet named Mauricio. I promised him when he touched down I would be in contact. He was present when I was blessed with my 3 branch stars. Three branch stars are elite stars for Vice Lords. It meant you were highly favored in the organization. In other words I was given some juice.

I was given fifty dollars, a bus ticket, and was driven to a Greyhound Bus Station 30 minutes up the road in Peoria. There were two other guys with me that had also been released. One guy was an older black man who had been locked up since the Seventies. I watched him closely as he took in the new world he knew nothing about. He stood firm isolated in a corner with a brown paper bag clutched tightly in his hand a cardboard box with his prison TV at his feet. In a way, I felt sorry for him and the tense look on his face told his story. The man had been locked in a cage for almost 30 years. The penitentiary was all he knew.

Since the bus didn't come until 12:30, I walked over to the convenience store with the other guy who was released with me. His named was Chuck and it turned out that he was from Joliet. We were headed to the same destination up North. I wanted to get out of the ridiculous choirboy outfit they dressed me out in. I had on a pair of black slacks and a short sleeve white button down. I bought a cheap black T Shirt that said Route 66. I guess anything was better than what I had on. We ended up sharing a 6 pack of Miller draft beer and smoked a real Cadillac. In the joint they call a Newport cigarette a Cadillac, because in the joint they were considered luxury and expensive just like a Cadillac. I couldn't wait to get on the bus and get back up North. I hated the South and being locked up in the South, the rednecks did not have a problem calling you a nigger.

Three days before I was released, The Orange Crush Unit came in, locked down the joint and took everything. The Orange Crush Unit was a group of Correction Officers used to restore order in the prison. They took can goods blue jeans gym shoes and anything they felt was a worldly influence on the inmates. If you were not in compliance they had no problem with beating the hell out of you. They now ran the joint and everything was in an uproar. All the top gang chiefs were removed. I guess their philosophy was if you cut the head off the snake the body would die. For years the Department of Illinois Corrections was run by the prisoners, now, the tables have turned.

They came in like a hurricane. We were forced to strip and bend over and cough then handcuffed and placed on the cold floor with nothing but our boxers on. A guy lying next to me said something slick, hearing him, the C.O. walked over and kicked him square in the mouth. The man's mouth instantly drew blood. For hours we laid out there on the cold floor while they turned our cages upside down.

I couldn't believe they treated human beings like this. This was unacceptable. Somebody had to speak out about this cruel and unusual punishment. I vowed I would contact the Governor or local representatives. But when I got out I was excited to be free and all of the good intentions I had went out of the window. I was only there for a short time but I had a lifetime of scars already.

I gazed out the windows lost in my own thoughts. I watched the beauty of a horse galloping in the wind. Life was so precious and at the same time we took it for granted. Bad things happen to good people every day and time keeps on moving. I wanted to do something extraordinary with my life I just didn't know what. As a kid, I used to dream about living in a big house like the Brady Bunch having a loving life and family where laugher and music comforted our home. I knew I had to find myself, but how could I, when the black raindrops were always falling on my head. I knew I had something special inside of me. Because whenever I set my mind to do something I'm always been successful. I just had to find my purpose before I self-destructed.

It was nightfall when the bus pulled in to the Joliet Greyhound Bus Station. I said my goodbyes to Chuck and wished him well. I had to get to Warrenville 12 miles away from Aurora. I was getting ready to pay for a cab but I saw a guy I knew from my town name Emmitt. Emmitt used to throw big parties in the town back in day.

"What up Emmitt?" I said giving him a dab.

"Man don't tell me you just got out," he laughed, eyeing my attire.

"Yup," I laughed along with him.

"Where you headed?"

"Man I'm trying to get to Warrenville to my Boss' house," I told him.

"Cool I'm about to run to the "A", I gotcha."

Man somebody upstairs was looking out, because I didn't know how I was going get to the land. We chopped it up as we rode. He shared with me he had just got out a year ago himself and he was living in Joliet above the Greyhound Station. I thanked him and handed him a ten-dollar bill and he went on his merry way. The very next day, I checked in with my parole agent. He informed me I had to see him once every month. It didn't take long for me to be back on the truck doing my thing in the moving business. One thing about me, I was never scared of any hard work. As long as you were showing me the money, I was there to collect it.

My first week out I got caught up in a snowstorm heading to Las Vegas to do a moving job. My boss was riding with me and he was drunk out of his mind. The roads were hazardous and this fool kept yelling drive faster. At one point he even mashed his foot over mines accelerating the truck into a burst of speed. Abandoned cars and trucks were everywhere. I never seen anything like this it was scary. One thing about my boss he was labeled a certified jackass. So I had to let him know. *Don't play with my life I'm trying to live.*

Due to the road conditions the highway eventually shut down so we had to find a hotel for the night. Thank God because honestly this man will push you to the point where you would want to put hands on him.

Las Vegas was all love sunny skies 80-degree weather. I was like a kid at Disney Land everything looked good. I've always had a strong appetite for desirable women and Las Vegas had plenty of them. We had two stops to make, one was in Vegas and the other load was San Diego. We were a day early so we decided to check into the Luxor Hotel. I chose the Luxor Hotel because it was 2Pac's favorite hotel. His death was still fresh and it still troubled me. To me Tupac Shakur was our modern day Martin Luther King, Malcolm X and Fred Hampton rolled in one. I found it profoundly appropriate to reflect on 2Pac hours before his untimely demise. 2Pac was more than an ICON he was a brother who was struggling with the same pain and hardship like so many other young black men in this country. We felt his pain that came from his soul. His music speaks the truth and you couldn't help but to respect it. So there I was standing on East Flamingo and Koval Lane pouring out a little Hennessey. 2Pac made the brown bottle appealing and I thought it was only right to pay homage to the fallen homie.

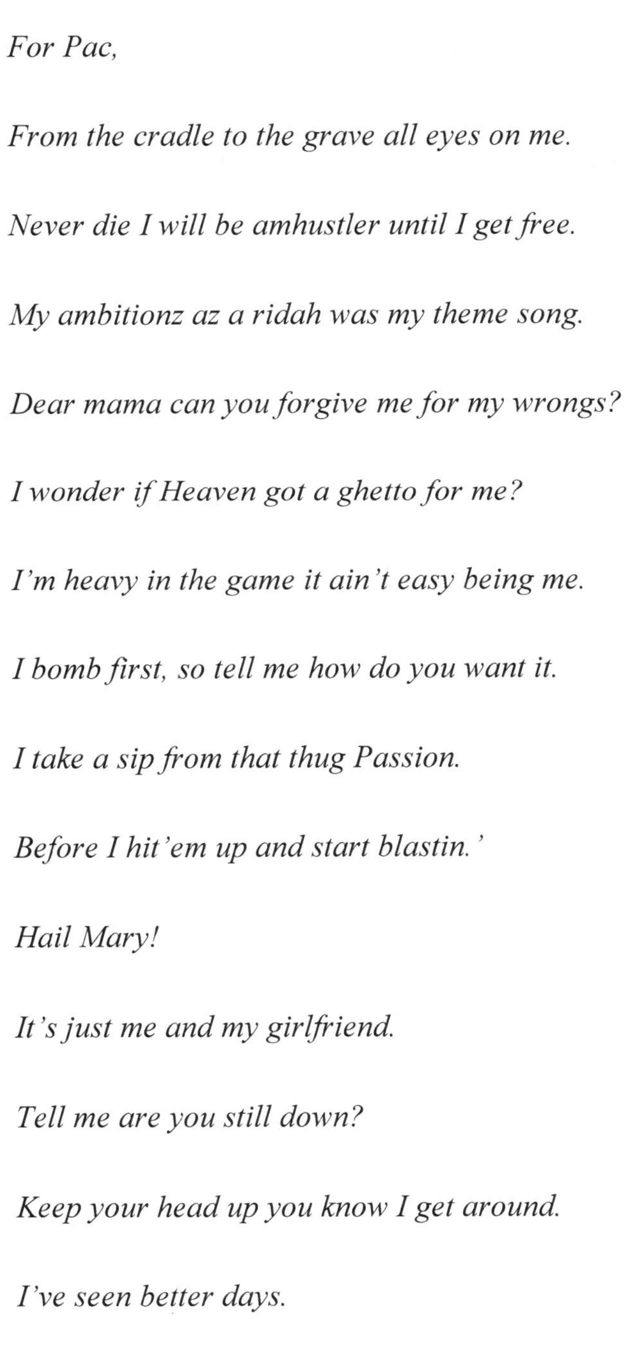

For Pac,

From the cradle to the grave all eyes on me.

Never die I will be amhustler until I get free.

My ambitionz az a ridah was my theme song.

Dear mama can you forgive me for my wrongs?

I wonder if Heaven got a ghetto for me?

I'm heavy in the game it ain't easy being me.

I bomb first, so tell me how do you want it.

I take a sip from that thug Passion.

Before I hit'em up and start blastin.'

Hail Mary!

It's just me and my girlfriend.

Tell me are you still down?

Keep your head up you know I get around.

I've seen better days.

Lord knows, I cry.

I shed so many tears in this life of sin.

If I die tonight will I win?

I'm under pressure you phony's don't know me.

They got me trapped.

I feel death around the corner.

I was learning in a hurry why they call Vegas Sin City. The things I did in Vegas, just put it this way, it will stay in Vegas. I already had addiction for sexy women and Vegas had some of the best. After a wild night in Vegas we headed over to Henderson, Nevada. Henderson was 20 minutes away. My boss's father and his brother Tommy lived there. The weather was crazy hot and I could care less for the dry heat. I couldn't imagine living out in the desert it felt like the blazing sun was shadowing you everywhere you went.

After I met everyone, I made myself at home. My boss's old man was down to earth and I liked him. But his brother Tommy was an out of this world character. He wasn't the sharpest tool in the barn and you couldn't wait to get away from him when he talked. I met all of Tommy's friends. They were hovering over an '83 Chevy Camaro in the garage. All of these guys were sort of wacky standing around telling stories about Area 51.

One of the guys claimed he used to work there and was very adamant that aliens were on display there. After a few more cans of beer, they began jonesing for crack. I guess since I was the only black in the room and was a known drug dealer they automatically assumed I would score them some drugs. I had to laugh because I knew nothing about getting dope in Las Vegas. But I was born a true gamer and believed I can always make things happen.

So there I was almost two thousand miles away from home trying to make a dollar out of fifteen cents. It was at least eight guys standing around in that garage I figure each had a hundred dollars in their pockets. If I could score a quarter or a half-ounce of crack cocaine it would be a nice come up on the West Coast. I took my boss's brother with me and drove their old man's Ford Escort back to Sin City. We rolled with all the windows down because the sun was hotter than a dog's dick. The Vegas heat was something else. At a red light I saw a man walk out of a gas station and pour a 2-gallon jug of water over his head.

When I got to Vegas, I went on Martin Luther King Dr. I figured every city I have been in, in the United States, black people lived on or off of King Drive. Las Vegas was no different. As soon as I hit the block, I was in the hood. It amazed me to see a part of Las Vegas you never saw on T.V. or in movies.

The Strip was minutes away but yet it seemed so far away. The message was clear as day. You people stay over here in your poor poverty stricken world and we will be over here in our magnificent rich world. I drove pass boarded up houses and abandoned buildings. To me it was no different from Chicago or any other black poor neighborhood in the country. Even though I was on a mission I always paid close attention to my surroundings and drew from my perception.

I knew my people wouldn't deal with me riding around with a white guy hanging out the passenger side window. Tommy reminded me of 2 year-old Toddler even though he was 32. So I had to shake him. The last thing I needed was to get caught up and never make it back home. No matter how many times I traveled outside the state of Illinois the goal was to always make it back home safely. I was born in the Chicago and I believe Chicagoan's have the ability to blend in anywhere. I ditched Tony in a nearby alley and ventured out on my own. I had on a fresh pair of Jordan's on and I took off my tank top to let them know I was hood. I walked up and down the block to see what was shaking. I bought a nickel bag of weed from a shorty who could've been no more than 12 years old. His clothes were dingy and when he spoke you easily could tell he was from the West Coast. Every other sentence had cuz in it. He pointed me into the right direction of what I was looking for, a house on the corner at the end of the block.

An older model boxed Chevy Impala was in the yard sitting on 20s. The car reminded me of back home because that's how we rolled. As I got closer to the small house a brown skinned black woman was sitting on the porch. Our eyes instantly locked she could haven't been no more than twenty-five.

"Aye what's good Shorty?" I hollered.

A sly smile curved her lips as she stood up and stretched. "I can tell you ain't from around here," she said easing off the porch.

"Why what gave me a way?" I replied with a lazy grin.

"Your swag different and plus nigga's around here don't workout. That body tho," she giggled, waving a hand in her face as though it were a cooling fan.

Shorty was thick and the short skimpy outfit she had on didn't hide what her momma had blessed her with. The attraction was there I couldn't deny it.

"So where you from?"

"Chicago."

"Chicago? I love Chicago," she smiled.

I cut to the chase and told her what I was looking for. She told me her boyfriend had just left to go re-up they only had a small stash left and he won't be back for a minute. She led me around back where there was a patio door. I followed closely behind her, two small children were eating popsicles and watching cartoons on a big screen television in the living room. She opened a kitchen cabinet and grabbed a roll of plastic baggies.

“How much you trying to spend?” She inquired.

“It depends on what you got.”

I could tell she was a little green to the game. Because there’s no way in hell I would allow strangers to walk in my house. We were flirting heavily and dipped off into the small bathroom. I must admit shortie had skills. I put it down for Chicago, before I gave her four hundred dollars for the rest of the stash that they had left. I was smiling all the way, back to the car, because I knew I was about to make some quick cash with 22 grams of crack cocaine I had stuffed in my pocket. For four hundred dollars I definitely got over and the extra sauce was icing on the cake.

Tim was sweating bullets when I got back to the car. The goofy grin he had on his chubby cheeks I could tell he was happy I made it back.

“What took you so long? He asked.

“Man hush,” I told him and pulled out of the alley.

All night long I had that small neighborhood in Henderson buzzing. Guys couldn’t believe crack cocaine was in their neighborhood. Turns out they didn’t mind smoking it, but they wouldn't dare get caught going to get it. They had career jobs and a reputation to protect. One guy thanked me and gave me an extra 50 bucks said he hadn't smoked crack in ten years. When it was all said and done I made a net profit of eighteen hundred dollars and the next morning I said goodbye to Nevada.

PAIN & ANGER

For the next few months I continued to work hard and check in with my parole officer. I was being a good boy; staying out the way. But that didn't last too long, because I had a short fuse. I hated people who were always trying to get over and my boss was becoming one of them. He figured he was the man because he had money and the power. He was Whitey and had no problem telling you that either. So he would play head games and play with your money.

For example, if he had a problem with you he would purposely cut you off of work until he felt you had suffered enough or kissed his ass wholeheartedly. *Who does that?* I explained to him on many occasions that he shouldn't play with other people's emotions. Guys wanted to put a real bad hurtin' on him; even some customer's wanted a piece of him. At times, things got so bad I wanted to choke him out. The man was putting me in a perplexed situation. Even friends of mine wanted to bash him and personally I couldn't blame them. Walt had his hands around the man's neck. This guy at times could be a jackass and I should've walked away a long time of go, but he was right he had the money.

The pain of my struggles kept me in a dark place. I couldn't shake loose the hounds that gave chase. Demons are real and they were starting to get the best of me. No matter how hard I would fight they would still overpower me. Every time I take two steps forward,

I get knocked three steps backward. I was frustrated and I was drowning myself with alcohol, drugs and women. When you feel pain you try to defuse it the best way you can. I was living on the road, without a home, it was just my bag and I. I had clothes spread out from house to house women were beckoning me to be their man. But I wasn't happy with my situation so being in a relationship was not going to happen. I was still unhappy with my circumstances. Pain and Anger seemed like they were willing to be my new friends.

We were back on the West Coast this time in Arizona. After we completed the job we were on our way headed back home on I-40 east. Out of nowhere my boss wanted me to stop by his Pop's house in Henderson, Nevada. Once we get there, he tells me he's flying back home. He claimed he had a meeting the next day. I just looked at him dumbfounded shaking my head. This guy never ceased to amaze me. He waited until we got all the way out here in the desert to drop this bombshell on me. He knew I had never driven out of state by myself. I've always had a licensed driver with me. This was another test that Doctor Evil was handing out. He gave me what he owed me and I drove off before I started to act real ignorant. One thing about me if I feel like someone is trying to play me I let them think their winning. But sooner than later I'm going to get at you.

Driving at night in the mountains is not a great idea, but I was trying to get far away from Doctor Evil as I could get. So many crazy thoughts were running through my mind. If I turned that truck back around all the penned up anger, I had inside was going to implode. Even though we were somewhat close; I knew it was a matter of time before I was next on his chopping block. So I had to make an exit route plan. That's what I was thinking the whole time I was driving in those pitched black mountains. To keep my mind from seething in anger and uncertainty I did what I always did, I prayed. Prayer was something I always believed in, because I knew Jesus was real. I always asked God for His protection and His mercy. Tonight was no different as the truck plowed through total darkness.

Voices fade as the cold water rose over my head. My body was drifting. I couldn't breathe.

The very next day I woke up in a cold sweat at a truck stop with the sunlight beaming in my face. I don't remember how I got here, but I was safe. I checked the time it was a quarter past seven west coast time. I stepped out the truck and stretched into an early morning yawn. Wow I was in Flagstaff about 250 miles outside Vegas. Now I needed to travel another 1600 miles to get home. I loved traveling on the road it was like being on vacation and getting paid at the same time.

Driving on the road gave me a piece of mind. I viewed it as therapeutic. It gave me a chance to escape my reality. When I was on the road, I was that little kid again staring out the window from the back seat, admiring the beauty of the unknown. The world was a big scary place, huge mountains, oceans and lakes. Demons still haunted you. It didn't matter who you were or what you looked like.

At times my life felt like I was trapped in a black hole and I couldn't escape. Other times I felt free as the birds of the air. I was always a free spirit different in many ways. I love to serve others and I believe goodness resides in every human being. Even the devil was once an angel. I did one more big job in the moving business before eventually my two worlds collided. In the late summer of '99, I took a good friend of mine to California. I loved to show brothers new experiences, because it was more to life than living in the hood. Most of them had never been anywhere but to Mississippi and back to Chicago. I wanted to show them it was a whole other world out here and they shouldn't be afraid to explore it.

We had a great time and on the way back home I lost a cashier check from one of the customers. I couldn't believe it. I never made a rookie mistake before and lost money. I was devastated, that check had half my pay in it. I will admit I had got sloppy and in my haste to show my friend a good time maybe I did a little too much. We got high off some marijuana we copped in Long Beach, California. I doubled back to the rest area where we slept in Arizona. Nothing. I called and told the boss man and he wasn't happy. My pockets were low and I knew we would run out of money for gas by the time we made it to Texas. I had to do something because I wasn't going to ask Doctor Evil to send me funds to get home. I made the mistake so I was going to have to deal with it. I had picked up a load from Long Beach that was schedule to be delivered to Glen Ellyn Illinois in two days. I was towing their minivan on a 15-foot trailer. I had big money on the truck I just had to make it home and save grace.

I have always been a hustler/survivor ever since I could remember. I knew I had to do something to stretch my funds. From New Mexico all the way to Missouri, we stole gas. It was quite an adventure I remember riding through Tulsa, Oklahoma and we had a blow out on the trailer. It was the middle of the night and everything was closed. This was turning into the trip from hell. We hopped a fence and found a tire that was a perfect match. The next morning, we got the tire repaired and we were on our way. A hundred miles outside St Louis the same tire blew again. Talk about bad luck. I had to stop on a hillbilly farm and pay 70 bucks for a used tire. The lesson learned? When you do wrong, it comes back to kick you in the ass.

As soon as we got back to Illinois we were running on fumes and somehow we managed to make it to Warrenville. My boss was waiting. He had a nonchalant attitude that I didn't too much care for. I see he bought a new 15-foot truck and he also sold his house. So he was rolling in the dough and refusing to give me my money.

"So you're telling me I have to wait until the lost check is voided and another one is reissued to get paid?" I asked.

"Yeah looks that way."

I shook my head in disbelief. I couldn't believe this guy. I drove half way around the country with no license risking my freedom. I was hot.

"Man pull over right now," I shouted with venom dripping from my mouth.

I had had enough! I was ready to beat his brains in. My friend tried to calm me down, but he knew I wasn't going. I had done so much for this man's business. Made him plenty of money and never cost him a dime. Everybody else had screwed up. They went to jail or they got the truck impounded. I was the only one who never cost him a penny. I always got the money and ran the show. Hell, I did it so well the customers loved to deal with me instead of him. I knew he wanted no part of me as we pulled into a small Mexican restaurant. After my temper subsided he gave me the old song and dance routine I often seen him give others before he stabbed them in the back. He tried to appease me by giving me half of my money and promising to pay me the rest when the check cleared. I was tired and frustrated all I wanted to do was sleep for a couple of days. Because being on the road was taxing and all you wanted do was complete the job and make it back home safely. It was clear to me this man didn't value me, and all the things I had done for him. The train had come to a stop and I knew I was being kicked off.

Y'ALL KNOW ME

Yeah! Y'all know me, Nowadays I'm like a household name. If you haven't heard of me you're either dumb or lame. However, in today's society I'm still rather inexpensive and I'm definitely not hard to find.

One taste of me, and you will lose your damn mind.

Sometimes, I come in a solid white substance, or if you're lucky, you can find me in that butter yellow.

But never mind the color, because I could get you higher than a mutha.

You see, in every ghetto across this great nation of ours I will always be relevant.

If you don't believe me, you can ask my father the government.

From my hood to your hood I tricked some of the best ghetto dimes

Into to doing white lines.

Now it is I------- who control their feeble minds.

I got them so strung out they'll do anything for another taste.

Even sell their ass or risk catching a case.

(After all I am worth it)

Yeah, y'all, know me.

But it don't stop there because I believe in equal opportunity.

You either serve or get served that's how I roll.

I got idiots everywhere from all walks of life puttin' in work for me.

They lie. Rob. Steal. Kill. Hustle and even go to the Penn for me.

Now that's GANGSTER!

I'm the real OG and I'm not going No Where.

Every place I go, people stop and stare.

I see the way they look at me. They can't wait to flame me up!

Or bag me up to get that paper.

I will always be a hot commodity.

Of course over the years other hardcore acts have tried to steal my thunder.

Foolishly thinking they could somehow take me under.

Lady Heroin. LSD. Mr. Ice. Tar Baby. Dr. Meth. Oxy C and Ecstasy

Just to name a few.

When it's all said and done and the smoke is clear, I am confident, I will still be

Shinning like the diamond I am.

I tell kids all the time I am not a role model, but if you're looking for that firer.

I will give you what your heart desires.

And, by the way I would like to personally thank some of you nice folks out there

Because without you I am nothing, but because of you I am legend.

So when you see me in the streets don't act like you don't know me

Get at me DAWG!

I'm always on the hunt for the next big Rock Star.

COLD-COLD WORLD

For weeks I heard nothing from Doctor Evil, but I did hear from others who said he was bad mouthing me around town. I mean this guy really didn't have a clue of who I was and what I was capable of doing. I knew I had a dark side to me that could be dangerous if provoked. Sometimes that frightened me and other times I welcomed it. If push ever came to shove, I had no problem with putting on that old suit I had stashed away in the closet.

With no job and no roof over my head I could call my own, I did what I had to do. I went back to peddling dope. One thing about dope you can always get what you want. You could walk in a house full of fiends and if you were the man with the big bag, the red carpet would be rolled out for you. You would be offered everything from a glass of water to a shot of ass. Women were notorious at using sex to get what they wanted and when it came to dope it wasn't any different.

Everything around me was moving at a fast pace and normally my right hand would know what the left hand was doing. But I was emotionally unstable and at times I couldn't get my bearings together. Looking back on it what I should've did was seek some type of counseling, because I was suffering from depression and didn't know it. I continued to drown myself with drugs, sex and alcohol. I was living for today and did not know what tomorrow was going to bring. Life was hard and at times unfair, but I couldn't see myself giving up no matter the struggle I had to find a way to stand back up again on my own two feet. You are a man before you are anything and that was a lesson I was learning the hard way. No one ever showed me how to be a man. Bubba always told me fight for what you believe in and never kill a man if you don't have to. All I wanted to be was successful, live, and do what I wanted. I was a dreamer. Sometimes I wished I could stay sleep and keep on dreaming.

In a blink of an eye my life was about to forever change and it was a change I wasn't expecting. One night I was at a bar in Du Page County. Some nights I would go in there and sell six packs of coke in the bathroom or in the parking lot. This particular night I was just chilling and throwing back a few beers and minding my own business. It was late when I walked out the bar into the parking lot and I noticed a white cargo van had eased up on me. It was traveling at a snail's pace.

"Hey buddy you got a light?" I heard a mellow voice call out.

I didn't say anything I just kept walking towards my vehicle. The van pulled up beside me and as I turned my head and a man pointing a gun at me leaped from the sliding door and shoved me in the van.

"Don't you move and get your fucking face down," the gunman screamed.

He searched my pockets while I was lying on the van's floor. I didn't have the slightest idea of what was going on. *Who? What? When? Why?* My mind was panicking in a frenzy mode. The van sped off and I could feel every bump along the way. I didn't know if I was going to live or die. Judging from my abductors, I knew they had to be the police. Some people would say how do you know? Being black you just know. I had enough interaction with the police in my life I could smell the pork cooking. The guy that shoved me in the van was about 5'10 white and of medium build. I didn't get a good look at his face. He had a dark ball cap pulled down tight around his eyes. The man behind the wheel said little but I did get a glimpse of the back of his head and I knew he was also white. I couldn't believe this was happening to me. I knew I done some bad things in my life, but no way did I deserved this.

My fate was up in the air and it seemed like hours had passed before the van had come to an abrupt stop. The door slid open making a horrifying sound that made my heart skip a beat. I was then ordered out with my hands up to the sky. I was told to walk forward and don't look back. I said a silent prayer waiting for the evident to take place. *Dear Lord don't let me go out like this.*

"Keep walking forward," the man with the gun said.

I trudged along with sweat poppin' off my forehead. I was headed towards a dark cornfield. My breathing was harsh and I could hear the pounding of my heartbeat against my rib cage. The fear of being in a situation where you have no control is unexplainable. My life was literary flashing before my eyes. I had guns pulled on me many times in my life but this was the unthinkable. My life can't end like this.

"Man I ain't walking no further if you going to shoot do what you gotta do," I said boldly.

For the life of me I don't know where those words came from. But I said them and stood firm.

"Oh so you're a tough nigger," the man with the gun spat angrily.

I stood silently with my hands still in the air waiting on his move. Suddenly, out of nowhere I could hear footsteps running towards me. Then I felt a hard blunt object strike me on the back of my head.

"You're not so fucking tough now are you? Consider this your lucky day. If I ever see your face again in that bar you will be one dead nigger." Then suddenly the gun discharged right next to the side of my head driving his point home. I lied there motionless. Frozen in time everything seemed unreal. I thought I was dreaming until I felt my own warm blood running down the back of my neck. My eardrums were ringing like an alarm clock was going off in my head. I blinked back angry tears as the van sped off into the night. I couldn't believe what just happen, some people might have been relieved to just be alive. But not me, black rage instantly filled my soul. It took me about three hours to walk back to my car. Those three hours were the longest three hours of my life. I still was in a daze of confusion and I had a monster headache, the worst I ever endured. I could barely focus trying my best to keep my eyes on the road. I knew I had to get as far away as possible.

I made it back to Aurora to a female friend's house. As soon as she opened the door everything turned black and I collapsed. I could hear her screaming trying to wake me up. My eyes popped open. "No hospital they trying to kill me," I mumbled. Then I faded out to darkness.

DARKNESS

Darkness holds this world like an iron fist; even the brightest star couldn't loosen its powerful grip.

I am alone imprisoned with the shadows I cast.

Darkness is the only one whom seems to feel my pain I shed from my past.

I'm breathing but I'm not living, my eyes are

Woke, but I can't see.

Is this going to be the death of me born into a world that doesn't give two cents about me?

I can't take the pressure nor the pain. Lord forgive me I'm going insane.

Jaded eyes low midnight approaches with Nowhere to go.

Sleep calls but it won't come easy.

I'm relentless at doing whatever it takes.

Darkness is not afraid of me it welcomes me.

However, the road I travel is paved in stone, no gold here, just a few dead bones.

Ain't no love here

It's every man for himself.

TAKER

My mind was made up and I was no longer going to sit on the sidelines and come in last place. The old suit in the closet was back on and it still fit perfectly. I had a 13 shot glock tucked in my waistband and I was ready for whatever. I had a plan and my plan was to take whatever I wanted by all means necessary. I was still angry about what had happened to me. I didn't tell anyone I just kept it to myself. Beside who was I going to tell, furthermore who would actually believe me.

I began to hang out with a white friend who I had known for a couple of years. He was a pretty low-key hard worker and stayed to himself. I could respect that because that's how I rolled. I was also his supplier when it came to the drugs he craved.

He had a lily white girlfriend; who was also sprung out on crack cocaine. I crashed over their place from time to time and they would get high until the sun came up. One thing about me I hated selling drugs. The only reason why I did it was because it was a way to make fast money. Some people wanted to make it a career, but I knew better, drug dealing didn't come with a 401K plan. I was a thinker and I had to think my way through these hard times. It didn't help the fact I started smoking a new drug called "Wet." Some call it happy sticks or (PCP). This drug was a powerful drug and it played on your emotions. Sometimes when I smoked this drug I felt like

Superman. Taking a cigarette or a joint and wetting it with abominable fluid was crazy so I guess you can call me crazy cause this was my new fix.

Secretly I began going back to the bar in Du Page County I wore a dreadlock wig with a dirty Oakland A's baseball cap. People I knew didn't recognize me. I was hoping to get lucky and run across my kidnappers, for what I did not know, it wasn't like I was a killer. But the way I felt anything was possible. I was on a whole 'nother level, so I isolated myself from my family as much as possible. I was in a very dark place and I didn't like the idea of someone telling me where I couldn't go. If I ever ran across them cowards again this time I was going to be ready. That whole experience had taught me a valuable lesson, "Never get caught with your guard down."

The TV was on and I've been locked in a hotel room for days brainstorming. Sometimes, you had to shut out the loud noise in your head to hear yourself to think. Besides, I loved staying up late watching old movies. It reminded of the good ole days where my grandmother (Ann Sullivan) and I would be engrossed in a James Cagney movie. Acting was something I knew I could be good at. I could watch Robert De Niro, Denzel Washington and Al Pacino movies all day.

For the next couple of weeks I began to put a master plan together. People wanted to hurt me so I was going to strike back and hurt them. But it was going to be their pockets. I wasn't going to take from my own. I was going to take from people who didn't give a damn about me. I was angry and I was seeking my justice. Everything that ever happened to me, from cops pulling their guns out on me, to white men throwing beer bottles at me or calling me coon or nigger; This was my payback I was going to show them all up.

My first job was easy a small storefront north of the city. I cased the joint for 3 days before I made my move. I never do anything on the spur of the moment, because a smart man always thinks before he acts. I always have to know the ends and the outs. Armed and ready I caught the manager exactly where I knew he would be, in the back counting money. My heart was pounding like a drum machine. I couldn't believe what I was actually doing. But there I was in character like a bad guy in countless movies I had seen many times before. In my mind the clock was ticking I had two minutes to be in and out. The manager's face twisted in horror as he stared down the barrel of a Chrome 357 magnum. I quickly had him shove all the money in a bag and promptly made my exit.

When I made my way back to my hideout, I closed the door and breathed a sigh of relief. It was over. The adrenaline rush had fizzled. I counted the money I had taken and I was not a happy camper. Even though it was thousands I could've had gotten much more. The bonehead mistake I made was I didn't get all the money that was in the safe. I was livid with myself. I calculated, it had to be a least ten grand I left behind. When you are taking a 6 to 30-year chance on a prison sentence you can't afford to make any mistakes. I had to get better and get better is exactly what I did. They say when you put your mind to do something you can do anything.

A week later I was on the move again this time I had struck gold. I made sure all the T's were crossed and my I's were dotted. No slip-ups it was a flawless victory. The money was piling up, but I still had emptiness within that I couldn't fulfill.

In the summer of July '99, I decide I would travel to New York. New York was a place I always wanted to visit. I had been there before just passing through but I didn't get a chance to enjoy the city. It was late in the evening when I arrived at La Guardia Airport. I must say I was impressed of the unique atmosphere of New York. The hustle and bustle of the huge city was intoxicating. I checked into the Conrad Hotel in New York, New York. I wanted to treat myself to the very best room they had to offer. When I arrived to my room I stretched out on the king size and made an invisible snow angel. The view from my window was breathtaking. New York City looked, better in person than it did on TV. I showered, dressed, and jumped in a taxi. I gave the driver three hundred dollars and told him to just drive.

We rolled through Time Square and I felt like a tourist staring up at the bright lights and the huge jumbotrons. The night was young and I was looking to get into something. I was in New York City and I was ready to make something happen. I had the driver drop me off at a nightclub he suggested in downtown Manhattan. Manhattan was an island near the mouth of the Hudson River. The club was a mixture of diversity. They played the latest hip-hop and pop hits. I mingled and wined and dined a couple females who were from Brooklyn. These sisters were party girls and they were also sack chasers. I understood their hustle because we all come from the same place. It's all about survival and when you are from the jungle you do whatever it takes to get out.

It was 4 am and these girls were nice and tipsy, so we headed back to my room and had a nightcap. I didn't go to sleep until they finally left my room the next morning. When I woke up I was ready to explore more parts of the city. One thing I didn't like about New York was the traffic. It seemed like we were stuck forever on the GW Bridge. I met this guy named Uptown he was a Jiffy. A Jiffy was an unlicensed cab driver who drove you wherever you wanted to go from their own vehicle. Uptown was a tall slim light skinned cat who, talked fast and every other sentence ended with *ya know what I mean*. He was funny and he got me some weed.

I had Uptown take me to Queen Bridge. I wanted to see were Nas was from. We shot past Nas' old neighborhood. It kind of reminded me of the projects in Chicago. The brothers were hanging out on the block like dirty laundry, the same shit different city. It was sad to see my brothers, completely stifled and stagnant. As we drove out of Queens, I couldn't help but think no matter how far a black man travels black rain will always be outside his window.

After spending a few days in New York I quietly creep back into town. Things hadn't changed; people hadn't missed me. I blew a wad of cash in NYC and I was ready to go back to work. I ran into one of my good brothers, Larry Huff. Little Larry and I go way back he had a heart of an lion and I can't say that for too many brothers that I know. When we were teenagers Little Larry had taught me how to hot-wire a car. It wasn't like I was interested but you never knew what Little Larry was on, he kept you on your toes. We chopped it up over a couple of beers as he wiped down his ride.

We had a fruitful conversation as we often did. Great minds think alike. One thing I always admired about Little Larry he was deep, same as his brother Duran. I remember when we were in the County Jail and he told me I had to get out of cell block 303 and I didn't listen to him. I ended up getting jumped by the folks and some of them had soap socks. Of course he had to rub that in.

It didn't take long for me to get back to doing what I do. But this time I was going to need some help. The stakes were high and I was ready to up the ante. My motto was do it big or don't do it at all. The next job I planned, I had a man on the door and one in the get-a-way car. I had an earpiece in my ear tuned into the police scanner station. If the police were on their way, I would know ASAP. This job was like taking candy from a baby everything went well. We scored a very well. Two days later I was in Atlantic City, New Jersey.

WHAT GOES UP MUST COME DOWN

I*'m drifting and drifting, voices are fading fast, my toes are dancing and the sandy water is rising over my head. I see the burning sun. Oh no, I can't breathe…*

I woke up in a daze of confusion with gun in my hand not knowing where I was until I saw the chain on the hotel door. I don't know how long I'd been sleep usually when I go to a hotel I go to rest. To be honest ever since that night of the abduction, rest was impossible, and I found myself smoking more "Wet." Paranoia was starting to settle in and unknown voices were coming from all over the place.

One night, I heard voices coming from the TV and it wasn't even on. Other nights I would see shadows and hear more voices outside my hotel room door. But when I open the door no one would be there. *Was I cracking up like a nut case? Or were the demons that gave chase getting closer?* Whatever the case was, I wasn't going to go cuckoo for cocoa puffs and these demons were not going to take me alive. Not just yet, I still had fight in me.

I did a couple more jobs and I realized being a taker is very addictive. It was turning into a drug I could never get enough of.

Every job I pulled off I did have a conscience. I would ask God for forgiveness and pray nothing went wrong. Sticking a gun in someone's face is risky business. You never know if a hero is in the establishment. Although my intentions were never to hurt anyone, that didn't always work both ways.

One night I was on a job and I came in guns blazing. I didn't have my crew but I've wanted to hit this place for a long time. Everybody was ordered to the floor; I counted 6 people and order the fat guy to open the safe. Out of the corner of my eye I noticed a guy lying on the floor moving his hand like a snake.

"Move again and I will put a hole in your head," I told him. Just out of curiosity I peeked around the corner to see what the man was reaching for and my eyes immediately leaped in fear. It was a good thing my mask was pulled down tight over my face because my mouth fell open like a garage door. On the bottom shelf next to a woman's purse sat a long nose black 44 revolver. The middle age man's face, redden as I stepped over him and plucked the gun from its hiding place. Now I had two guns and I meant business.

"Down. Down. Down. Don't nobody move," I shouted.

I tossed a woman a bag and I had her quickly empty the safe. She was nervous clearly shaken. I assured her as long as she did what she was told everything would be fine. It was important to be a very good actor because that's all I was doing. Acting. After she did what she was told, I hauled ass and didn't look back. I was two minutes away riding in the back of a van when I heard through my earpiece the police had been dispatched. I always stayed two steps ahead of the boys in blue. That's one of the reasons why I never got caught.

My old crew and I had to part ways they were getting too sloppy and greedy. Now I had to use the white boy and his job was to drive. They wouldn't be looking for a white guy so my plan worked to perfection. All he wanted was crack and I took care of him. He needed rent money? Done. He needed money to get his van fixed? Done. He never saw a gun, or knew what place I was going to hit. His job was to drive no questions, because if I ever got pinched he wouldn't know anything details.

After the big job I now had enough money stashed to do something with. I could open a business or buy my momma another house. I hated the fact she lost her house because of me. That always tore a hole in my chest. I had made up my mind I was through with armed robberies. My Jesse James outlaw days were over. I wanted to take a trip out west to California to see a female friend named Tonya. I met Tonya in Long Beach at a gas station she worked at. She was good people and we always kept in touch.

The night I was leaving to go to California I stop by Huntington to see my babies. Sharon showed me a picture of her and some boy hugged up I made a mental note I was going investigate that when I got back. My 7-year old son was outside running wild with his shirt off. Sherece was being Sherece, she had her hand out wanting some money. I didn't have much money on me, but I gave them what I had. On my way out, I saw ZO (Alonzo Verge). I hadn't seen him in a minute it was good to see that brother. He was a good dude.

I stayed 5 days in sunny California. Tonya and I had a blast. Tonya reminded me of a young Jada Pinkett. She was feisty and easy on the eyes. We vibe well together and we loved to put the chronic in the air. Her mother was trying to get me to move to Cali and at the same time batting her eyelashes at me behind Tonya's back. Her mother was a trip. She had a boyfriend younger than me, and everything she wore was spandex. She said she didn't date guys her age; she needed more than ten minutes. Although I liked Tonya a lot, I just didn't see her in my future. Hell I couldn't see me in my own future. She always kept asking me where did I see myself in the future? That was a really good question and to be honest I didn't know the answer. I just wanted to be happy and successful. I saw so much and I've been through so much. Sometimes when I wake up I can't believe I'm still here.

Before I left, I bought Tonya a used Toyota Camry she had two small kids and one was a boy named Jamar. Jamar had Autism. Autism is a neurodevelopmental disorder characterized by impaired social interaction, verbal and non-verbal repetitive behavior. She had a hard time dealing with the fact that her child wasn't normal. She was very good mother and she always put her kids first. Her kid's father had been killed in South Central so it was tugging on my heart to do something to help lessen her woes. We all need help sometimes and I was happy to give her something she could use instead of public transportation. Her warm wet tears showed her gratification. The very next day she dropped me off at the Airport. That was the last time I saw her.

It was cold and windy, late in the afternoon when I returned home. I caught a cab from Chicago's Midway Airport back home to Aurora. I had to wait for the white boy to get home so I could get my money. I had secretly stashed it in an old vacuum cleaner hidden in the crawl space. I was feeling a little shaky and I hated waiting. I was sitting on the front porch when I noticed two unmarked police cars coming down the street at a creepy crawl. Immediately my antenna when up.

One of the plainclothes detectives was a woman I knew. She was from Du Page and the other was an Aurora PD. Both cars pulled in the parking lot when they observed me. My first thought was to run they finally caught up to me. I tried to remain calm and not look suspicious. They began asking all sorts of questions. Who I was? How tall was I? Where is your buddy?

Of course I played dumb, but I knew they had something. They began searching me and in my Newport cigarette box I had a wet stick in there. I watched closely as he scanned the box and then placed it back on the hood of the car.

“Do you have any anything in your pocket that’s going to poke me,” he asked?

“No sir,” I replied.

He reached in my pocket and pull out about a thousand dollars. “Looks like you had a good night.”

I ignored him and kept a train eye on the woman detective she was on her phone. Things certainly didn’t look good. Then the white boy and his girlfriend pulled up in the van. I was livid looking at this clown sideways. If I saw him talking to the police outside my house, there’s no way I would’ve stopped. As soon as he got out the van they put the cuffs on him and arrested him. They claimed he had an old warrant. I knew that was a lie. They had something, but what?

“Excuse me sir am I free to go? I asked.

“Well we would like to speak with you down at the police station.”

I looked at him like he was crazy there was no way in hell I was going to the police station if I wasn’t in handcuffs.

“Am I under arrest?

“No.”

“Well, I’m not going to the police station. Whatever you have to say to me you can say right here.”

“We don’t discuss our business on the street.”

I looked him in the eye. “I don’t discuss my business at no police station.”

“Look whoever talks first you know gets the deal.”

“Sir I don’t know what you’re talking about. If I’m not under arrest can I go?”

Two more Detectives had showed up and they were looking upside my head. I looked over at the white boy and he had a confused look on his face. *I was thinking what an idiot he was. He didn’t see the big picture. He didn’t have any warrants they wanted to get him down to the police station and drill him about arm robberies.*

“You’re free to go, but if I were you I would reconsider and come with us and try to resolve this matter.”

“You guys are scaring me. I will be at my lawyer’s Fred Morelli’s office,” I quickly said trying to get the hell out of there.

I stepped inside the apartment and schooled the white boy’s girlfriend about what was going on. She now had a worried look on her face. My mind was on my money. I slid open the crawl space door and hurried to the old vacuum.

"Hey J what are you doing down there?'

I paid her no attention and quickly unzipped the bag that contained my money. Stacks of thousands of dead Presidents were staring at me in the face. Then there was the pounding of the door. My heart raced in fear as beads of sweat began poppin' off my forehead like Shaquille O Neal on the line ready to shoot free throws. I quickly stuffed a couple of stacks in the boots of my Timbs and zipped the vacuum bag back up. I peeked out the window and observed the white boy signing a paper on the trunk of the unmarked car. A cop had his gun drawn standing at the side of the door. I slowly open the door.

"Let me see your hands," The cops said.

"Man what's going on?" I said with my hands touching the sky.

"There's a gun in here we're just taking precaution."

I was shaking like a leaf because I did not know what this fool had told them. He had obviously given them permission to search his home, which I thought was stupid. The man had all sorts of get high tools in the house. I gave him a disgusted look and his eyes fell forward. At that moment I knew this could get ugly, because he could rat me out if push came to shove. When the police told me I was free to go! I hightailed out of there as fast as I could.

I couldn't believe that I was walking away from the scene. Every few seconds, I would look back to see if I was being followed. I walked to Marywood, just up the block away on Farnsworth and called for one of my most trusted friends to come get me out of dodge.

I was paranoid, I just knew they were going to jump out the bushes and nab me.

Once my friend showed up she took me down to see my Attorney Fred Morelli. Fred was known as "Freedom Freddy" and over the years he had freed me many of times. He gave me stern advice after calling down to the police station. Morelli told me the white boy had been in the interrogation room for hours. He was probably in there singing like a canary. I had given Morelli some money to keep the wolves off of me. He suggested I lay low but he also warned me if the white boy fingered me the cops would be back.

I left Morelli's office feeling dejected and my mind was all over the place. I needed to get my money out of that house. I had somebody drive past the house and they said the police were still there. I didn't know what I was going to do, if I couldn't get my money. I waited until midnight only to find out the police had left and my money was gone. My heart sank to the pit of my stomach. I couldn't believe what was happening. I knew now they were going to definitely be coming after me. But sixty thousand dollars was going to be a hard pill to swallow. I had no time to sit and waddle in the mud what was done was done. I had to get on the move before the walls of Jericho came tumbling down.

ON THE RUN

It was 2 AM and sleep was yet impossible. I had one of my guys drop me off downtown Chicago. I had to get out of town on the first thing smoking. I didn't know where I was going or what I was going to do. I just had to get somewhere safe and think. I walked across the bridge on Canal Street with a duffle bag thrown over my shoulder. The cool breeze coming from the Chicago River felt appeasing against my face. I aimlessly walked the streets downtown with my head hung low thinking of my next move. When it came to my life I thought all along I was playing chess, but in reality I was playing checkers. All I kept thinking about was the money I left behind. It was clouding my thoughts.

I headed towards Greek Town and I met a guy named Shorty. Shorty was an older guy in his late forties. He wore a huge smile carrying a fresh Chicago Sun Times Newspaper. It was something about his warm spirit that drew me into him. I had a canny third eye and I could always tell the good and the bad in people. Shorty was homeless and I could tell by his demeanor he got high. He confirmed that he sometimes lived on Lower Wacker sleeping along the bridge. I needed a room to get off the streets.

"Hey Shorty you got an ID?"

"Yup," Grinning and digging in his pocket pulling out a State ID.

"Check it out I need you to rent me a room I will pay you."

"Cool, I gotcha brother."

We went inside the Quality Hotel in Greek town and the black lady at the front desk claim they only had double beds left. I knew that was a lie because the parking lot was half empty. After talking to Shorty for a hot minute he told me he did over twenty years in prison and there was no way he was going back. If he had to live on the streets for the rest of his life at least he won't be locked up in a cage. The whole time I was talking to Shorty I couldn't help but feel some sort of compassion for him. All he wanted was to be free and enjoy the simple little things in life. Although I didn't agree with his philosophy, I did respect his truths. I thanked him for renting the room and handed him two hundred in cash. To my surprise he kept sixty dollars and returned the rest.

"Man, I won't be needing all that," he smiled heading to the door.

"You sure brother?"

He paused and glared at the folded Andrew Jacksons he had in his hand. "Yeah man, I'm sure and I thank you. And whatever you're running from, may God be with you."

I stepped out on the balcony of 12th floor and fired up the Wet stick I had left in the box of Newport's. I inhaled deeply. The loss of sixty grand was all I could think about. *Man I was stupid! That money could've came in handy, to help pay my Attorney fees.* A black man with no money fighting the justice system was a no win situation. I had over four thousand dollars in cash and I had to leave Illinois. In my mind, I was a born hustler and I could go anywhere and get money. But I hated to leave like this. I was restless and I couldn't sit still long enough to think clearly.

5 a.m. had rolled around and I had made my way to Union Station located on Canal Street. Chicago Union Station was a massive iconic train station with commuter rail lines, plus shops and eateries. As a kid, I spent a lot of time here traveling back and forth to the city. I loved riding on trains. It always gave me a sense of calmness. I didn't know where I was going, but I wanted it to be somewhere I never been before. I stared up at the board and studied the time of the early departures. The West Coast was out of the question. I was leaning towards the East Coast and the city of brotherly love is where I punched my ticket.

I boarded the Amtrak and we were off at 6:13 AM sharp headed to Philadelphia, Pennsylvania. Everything went smoothly. I went straight to my suite on the train and immediately locked the door. I wasn't trying to trust anything or anyone. I had a pistol in my bag and I was now a wanted man. I felt like I was playing a character on an episode of *The Fugitive*, everything seemed so surreal. In a blink of an eye my life was turned upside down and I had no one to blame but myself. I glanced out the window as the train began to pick up speed. I thought about my love ones and the embarrassment that I was going to cause them. *They say what you do in the dark will surely come to the light. I was starting to become a believer. Sweet Home Chicago, I was going to miss.* I pulled the shade down to block the sunlight from my worried eyelids that were heavy. The sandman had finally come.

HOW CAN I

H*ow can I fly high, when I'm afraid to try?*

How can I believe in something, when I'm use to nothing?

How can I move on, when I keep hearing the same song?

How can I stand strong like a man, when no one gave the plan?

How can I bury the past, when I still want to kick somebody's ass?

How can I give love, if no one's there to receive it?

NO WAY OUT

When I opened my eyelids, the train had stopped in South Bend, Indiana. For the first time in 24 hours, I felt a little sense of relief sweep over me. I knew whatever was coming my way eventually I was going to have to deal with it. But it wasn't going to be today. I figured once I stacked some more paper, I would return to Illinois and deal with what I had coming. To be honest I had no plans to run forever, but I would be a damn fool to face the music especially when I wasn't ready. I unfolded a thin blanket and threw it over my frame. I was still tired. To stop all the madness going on in my head; I had to turn the lights out.

It was 5:15 pm when the train rolled into Pittsburgh, Pennsylvania. I stretched into a lazy yawn, grabbed my bag, and stepped out to grab a burger. I wasn't really hungry but I had to eat something so I forced the choke burger down. The train wasn't leaving for another half hour, so I wandered around downtown Pittsburgh out of boredom. To my surprise, I found the Steel City alive and full of energy. Immediately, I was sucked in and captivated by my surroundings. Pittsburgh was nowhere near as big as Chicago, but it had character. Right then and there I decided I was going to change the plan and stay in Pittsburgh. For some strange reason my spirit was telling me this is where I was supposed to be.

I paid a guy 20 bucks to take me to a low-key spot. He took me to a place called the Avalon Motel. It was just outside of Pittsburgh overlooking the Allegheny River. Immediately, I thought the place was perfect. I got a room, settled in, and took a long hot shower. After putting on some fresh clothes, I walked over to the bar/restaurant next door. I was getting a feel of the place and it didn't take long to figure out I was in a goldmine for drug activity. The place was crawling with fiends. Young white girls were strung out on crack cocaine and heroin. They looked like something out of The Walking Dead. I never saw anything of this magnitude back home. Everyone who I had made contact with was on something. So I threw my hat in the ring and jumped right back into game. I needed money so I had no choice.

For the next few days I set up shop in one room and slept in another. I had a white guy named Dave and his black girlfriend Tasha running the operation. For the most part everything ran smoothly until I ran out of dope. Getting a high amount of quality drugs for a decent price I see was going to be a problem. Back home the cocaine was ten times better and I didn't have any trouble finding what I was looking for. Pittsburg was different you had petty nickel and dime dope dealers whom were all for themselves. Plus, it didn't help the fact I was from Chicago. I was the last person they wanted to see shine. It's something about Chicago, when traveling to different parts of the country they either loved you or hated you.

I was on a mission to make things happen. I wanted to make as much money as possible so I could return home and turn myself in. Anyway that was my goal. Finally, I came in contact with a good connect. His name was Dog Nutz.. Dog Nutz was a Crip from Cali and he was confined to a wheelchair. He was a small, little dude who resembled DMX. He told me he had been shot and was paralyzed from the waist down. The doctors said he would never walk again. I admired his strength. He was a strong dude. He had a pretty young girlfriend who stood by his side. Her name was Kara everyone called her Kay-Kay. She was definitely a sweetheart with soft brown features. Dog Nutz kept a close eye on her.

After I got back in power, I rushed back to the motel to cook up two ounces of cocaine. When it came to cooking up cocaine; I was a mad chemist. I took a small pot and placed it over the hot plate like stove. I added water to the pot and placed a pickle jar with water inside of it. All eyes were on me. These fiends probably never seen, this much dope at one time. So I was watching them very carefully. I was a long way from home and plus I was not comfortable with folks I did not know. I added ten grams of coke and a couple teaspoon of baking soda, and stirred the cloudlike mass with a butter knife I made into a stem. I added cold ice water and immediately the dope turned solid and crack cocaine was born. I repeated this process until all the dope was cooked up.

It didn’t take long for the word to get around the motel that a new sheriff was in town. I had them running back for seconds and thirds. For the next few days the money was starting to pile up and the hate on the face of some of the local cats was real. I carried my glock on me everywhere I went. I didn't trust a soul. These cats where known to nickel and dime their customers, where I'm from I was taught to give plenty and treat the people who shop with you with respect because respect goes a long way. So quite naturally my clientele went through the roof.

Late one night I got a phone call that a guy in the smoke room was spending a lot of money. So I got up to go check him out. When I walked into the room the guy was geek and couldn't stop twitching. I introduced myself as Chicago and began to have a conversation with the man.

"So my man are you from around here? I asked.

He nodded taking another blast from his pipe.

I watched him closely and he appeared to be no different from any other smoker I seen who got high. He was a short, stocky, light skin brother with kind eyes. The white boy and his black girlfriend were high out of their rabbit minds, knowing them they probably smoked up half the man's dope.

"Aye Chicago," the man whispered in a low voice. I moved in closer pulling up a chair at the small round wooden table. "What can I do for you my man?"

He slowly swallowed the lump in his throat and tried to speak, but nothing came out. He then reached in his pocket and laid ten crisp twenty-dollar bills on the table. I motion for the white boy to come here. He showed me what we had left in the stash and I told him to give it to him. The white boy looked at me like I had lost my mind. I didn't care about holding on to dope and penny pinching people out their hard earn money. The man had spent over a thousand dollars with me. As far as I was concerned, the man could have what he wanted.

Three days later I tried to reach Dog Nutz to re-up, but the man was nowhere to be found. So I had to settle on whatever I could get. I took a couple L's then made a gamble I should never, had made. I met a cat named New York. He was a tall, dark skinned brother who always wore a New York Yankee hat. Right away I didn't trust him. The man talked fast and he had the coldest dark eyes I've ever seen. He had two flunkies with him all the time and both of them looked like they needed a shower. This chick named Gail from the Chi had hooked me up with him. I met her and her girlfriend Marie at a bar when I first arrived in Pittsburgh. I told the man I was looking for an eighth of a key. A eighth is basically four and a split. On the night of the pick-up, I arrived at the apartment complex where New York told me to meet him. I had mixed feelings about the whole set up. I had Gail driving and a guy named Big Lowe was riding in the back seat. Both of them were smokers and all they wanted to do was get high.

I pulled out my Glock and jacked one in the chamber and stuffed the gun in my waistline.

Gail gave me a concern glare. “Oh my god! Why do y’all carry guns? I hate guns! I’ve seen too many deaths in Chicago of gun violence that’s why I left.”

I didn’t bother to respond because she sounded like a bird talking outside of her neck. When you in the game and you cared about your life, you had no choice but to carry a gun. I exited the vehicle and headed up the stairs to apartment #D. As soon as I knocked on the door, one of New York henchmen let me in.

“Chitown, Chitown was good son?” New York said as I entered the apartment.

I gave him a nod and followed him to the kitchen. I sat down with my back against the wall I wanted to be in position so I could see everything. The kitchen was small and smelled like someone just fried pork chops.

“I got that butter for Chitown this from up north son,” he stated handing me a zip lock back.

I took possession of the plastic bag and examine the merchandise. There were 4 1/2 ounces of cocaine. It was all shake no solid. New York watched me carefully as I busted down one of the bags and tasted the white powdery substance.

"Man look at you Chitown, you on your business," he smiled wickedly.

I was satisfied as my tongue instantly became numb. I eye balled the size of the package and the weight looks about right. I tossed him thirty-eight hundred dollars and watched him count it. No doubt he taxed me on the merch because back home I would never pay that kind of price for a four and a split.

"Munchie," he called out and handed a large woman the money. Her eyes sweep over me momentarily as she exited.

I cuffed the dope and stuffed it in my jacket, and I was on my way. New York walked me to the door and gave me a pound and I was out. I thought it was strange he didn't extend an invitation on a re-up considering he just juked me out of hundreds.

As soon as I got outside huge raindrops begin falling. I pulled my hoodie over my head and open the door to step out. Suddenly out of nowhere I felt something hard strike me with brute force on the side of my head. I stumbled forward in a daze of confusion, but I wouldn't allow myself to fall. Everything around me moved in a blur and the ringing in my left ear sound like a fire alarm was going off. The next pain I felt sent me crashing to the wet asphalt. Everything went black. I faded out.

WHEN IT ALL FALLS DOWN

When my eyes popped open I didn't know where I was. I had a headache out of this world. I tried to sit upright but it was no use my brains were scrambled. I was lying on a couch on my backside. There was a TV on, and I could see Stuart Scott on the ESPN Sports channel. *Where am I? What happened? How did I get here?* I had so many questions without answers. I needed my questions answered to stop my heart from racing like a locomotive. With all the strength I could muster, I manage to sit upright. I felt the side of my head and there was a huge knot.

"Aye Gail he up," Big Lowe said coming into the living room.

"Oh my god, Chicago. Are you okay?" She inquired kneeling down beside me.

"What happened?"

She paused turning her eyes away from me. "They robbed you. I don't know who they were it all happened so fast."

I began to slowly replay what I could remember before I blacked out. Everything started to add up and I believed I was set up.

"Did they get my gun?"

"No! They didn't get that it was stuck in your pants leg."

"Where is at?"

"Here it is," Big Lowe said handing it to me wrapped in a paper bag.

I stared at them suspiciously. I didn't know what to think or who to trust. "How long have I been out?"

"You been out for hours you might need to go to the hospital. I think you have a concussion," Gail answered.

"No, I don't need to see no doctor," I quickly said, "I just need a moment to sort all this out.

"Oh I hate to tell you this, but they broke into your room at the Avalon and stole all your stuff."

"Gail, tell me that ain't so."

"I wish I could. Big Lowe and I went over there last night and Ronny was putting a new lock on the door."

"Yeah bruh they cleaned you out good," Big Lowe added.

I sat there with my head hung low. My brain was racing with murderous thoughts. *If someone hurts you, you hurt them back.* That's what I was taught. I never in my life killed anyone but I would be lying if I never thought about it. I believe there comes a time in everyone life when get back is necessary. Turning the other cheek wasn't going to happen. "Do anybody, know I'm here? I asked.

"No we didn't tell nobody," Gail replied.

Two days had gone by and I was back up and running. I had enough of sleeping on Gail's worn out couch. It was time for me to do what I do. I had her drop me back off at the Avalon. I could tell she was happy I was leaving her little pathetic life. The money had run out and the dope was gone; so I was the last person she wanted tagging along. It's funny how your life can change in a blink of an eye. I went from a hundred to zero in three short weeks. On top of the fact I had a multiplex of outstanding warrants out on me. A wise man once told me if you wanted to stop digging yourself a deep hole, put down the shovel.

I sat in the shadows watching everything that moved from a window in the northeast corner of the motel. An old shabby looking white guy who resembled Willie Nelson had no problem with letting me using his room as a stakeout. I told him when I got back in power, I was going to throw him an eight ball on GP. He was so delighted to hear that the whole time I was there; his face was lit up like the morning sun.

After I had seen enough, I made my way over to my former workers' room. Just as I was getting ready to knock on the door, the white boy, Dave, swung open the door.

"Oh um hey Chicago. I was just going to bum a couple of smokes. Um c'mon in," he smiled weakly.

"Chicago," Tasha waved taking a drag from a cigarette.

"Man, bro, sorry what happened Tosh and I tried to find out who broke into your room and stole your stuff. But man no one knows anything."

"Yeah when went up there to check the whole room was tore up," Tasha chimed in.

Dave gave her an uneasy look and I sat back and nodding my head listening to everything they had to say. I was far from boo boo the fool, but I let them continue to see how far they were willing to go. From what I was told Dave was the prime suspect. He was seen selling a couple pair of Air Jordans. I waited for him to step out the room so I could be alone with Tasha. I knew I could turn her. She was a weak link.

I pulled out my glock and placed it on the table. Tasha glanced at it like it was a snake. She excused herself and went to the bathroom. When she returned, she kept fiddling with her hands and sat on the edge of the bed. I eased out of the chair that was next to the round wooden table and held my gun by my side. "You got three seconds to tell me everything or I won't be responsible to what is about to happen to you."

Tasha's face twisted in fear. She had a right to be afraid because what I really wanted to do to her, God help me. "Okay. Okay. Okay. But it was Dave and Dog Nutz. They did it!" she said in a skittish tone.

"Dog Nutz, was in on it?" I questioned. "How he in a wheel chair?"

"Chicago, I told Dave he was wrong, but he has a mind of his own."

Right on cue, Dave walks into the room. He looked at me then at Tasha. Her head fell. He knew and quickly turned on his heels trying to tear the hinges off the door attempting to flee. In one motion, I was all over him like a bad cop. I hit him with everything I had then dragged him away from the door. I straddled him and smacked him with the pistol several times until he drew blood.

"Oh you wanna steal from me? After all I did for you?" I yelled and continue to pound his face unmerciful. I could hear Tasha piercing cries in the background. "Please stop Chicago! You gone kill him!" she sobbed.

Breathing heavily, I stood up and order them to give me all the money they had. Everything I had was now gone and my soul was raging with burning fire. They gave me a lousy $33.00! I crumbled it up and I stuffed it in Dave's mouth. Armed with all the information I needed, I was off to pay Dog Nutz a visit.

When I knocked on Dog nutz door, I could hear loud rap music. Kay Kay finally opened the door. I stepped in and noticed two guys I did not know sitting at the table. Dog Nutz was sitting in his wheel chair stuffing weed in a cigar. I could see it in his eyes he was surprised to see me.

"What up, Chicago?" He chuckled.

Kay Kay closed the door behind me and I didn't waste no time to pounce. I hit Dog Nutz with a wild right hook, sending him crashing to the floor. At gunpoint, I made everybody empty their pockets. The bastard even had my Oster hair trimmers plugged up in the wall. I took all their money, drugs, and collected a 38 special. Some might say I was wrong for what I did. But when you're living wrong, wrong don't recognize wrong. I made my way down to Willie Nelson's room and handed him a handful of drugs that would keep him high for a couple of weeks. He had tears of joy in his eyes. "Chicago you have always been good to me," he beamed.

"Take care of yourself old man. I will see you around," I said before disappearing into the night.

REVENGE IS THE SWEETEST JOY

I waited in the wee hours of the night to make my next move. I wiped the cold rain away from my eyes as I patiently sat outside of New York's spot. I hid in the shadows on the side of his apartment about 150 feet away. I had on all black clothing and a mask covering half of my face. Pay back was in order and I was ready to go all out. *A man who has nothing has nothing to lose.*

With keen eyes I closely watched New York and his wanna be goons every move. Every so often New York would come out and spark a blunt and go back upstairs. It took everything in me not to fire off some shots in his direction. But I had to remain calm, cool, and collected I couldn't let my emotions overwhelm me.

It was 4 a.m. and it was time to make my move. Everything was rather quiet. The rain had stopped and the fiends must've, ran out of money because suddenly they stopped coming. I gazed up at the second story window of New York's baby momma's apartment; the lights were finally off. I eased up the stairs. When I got to the second floor I could see shadows moving.

"Aye what you need?" A voice called out walking towards me. As he approached, I could see it was one of New York's stunt dummies.

"I need a fiddy piece," I replied with my head hung low.

"A fiddy?" He said anxiously.

As he moved in closer I quickly drew my gun. "Get them hands up and don't move," I snarled at him. The man's dark eyes grew large in fear as he realized what was happening. "Man what you on?" he asked.

"What does it look like I'm on? Empty them pockets before you catch a hot one."

I watched the man with careful eyes as he pulled out a wad of cash. As soon as I snatched the money from his hands, New York's tall slender frame came juddering out of the apartment.

"Aye, I'm gettin' jacked!' The man yelled and took off running down the hall. New York peeped the demo and immediately started shooting at me. I hid behind the stairwell and sent loud shots back in his direction. This was like something out of a Wild-Wild West Movie. I couldn't believe I found myself embattled in a gunfight. New York headed outside and I followed. I could hear New York's baby mama screaming outside the upstairs window. She voiced her displeasure that she was going to lose her place. I pressed on like a soldier at war and fired more shots at New York as his tall frame zig-zag through the wet parking lot.

He hid behind a car and squeezed off three rounds at me. I took cover and dove in between two parked cars. I was lucky he was a horrible shooter because he had me dead to the right but missed wildly. I stayed on the ground breathing heavily as more bullets ricocheted off of the parked cars. In the distance, I could see his feet moving. “One of y’all bring me that mack,” he yelled.

Quickly I jumped on my feet and peeked over a car. *I think he’s out of ammo.* I fired two quick shots over the car and New York took off running. I took off after him, watching him slip and fall, and get back up again. I was closing in fast with brazen foot speed as he dipped behind a building and ran through the back yard. He cut another sharp corner and this time he was down for the count grimacing in pain. He had run into a heap of garbage spilling over the cans. I eased up on him with my pistol aimed at his head. He slithered wildly on his back like a snake trying to get loose. I fired a round into the ground just missing his right leg. He paused in his tracks and slowly turned his head towards me.

“Man whatcha want? I got money, here take it’” he said in a hurried tone pulling out bundles of rubber banded money.

Personally I could care less about the money. I wanted to punish this fool for having me set up and robbed by his clown crew. *It ain’t no fun when the rabbit got the gun.* I reached down and scooped up the money then I dropped kicked him in the side like I was kicking a football. Immediately he grabbed his rib cage, and let out a sharp cry. I tried to kick him again but this time he held out his arm to help soften the blow.

"Dog, I gave you the money don't shoot me," he pleaded.

Pointing the gun at his head, I so badly wanted to squeeze the trigger. I have met a lot of bad guys in my life, but this cat rubbed me the wrong way. Not to mention he just tried to kill me. I was so hot that smoke was coming out my ears. In my anger, I let off two quick shots and got out of dodge. I could hear police sirens in the background getting closer. My heart was racing a mile a minute as I ran like a deer in the wind. God didn't make me a killer, but the anger in me wanted to be that killer.

Twenty minutes later I was back at the Avalon Motel. I was still raging. I saw the fear in New York's eyes as he stared down the barrel of death. The two shots I let off missed his head purposely. I just couldn't force myself to be something I was not. The angel of God had reasoned with me, because had he not I would've made a mistake I couldn't come back from. As I paced back and forth in Willie Nelson's tiny room the devil would not let loose of his threshold on me. My mind was racing with crazy thoughts and even the fragile old man was shaking in his boots. He kept watching me pace back and forth as though he was checking out a tennis match.

I fired up a wet stick and allowed the foul smelling substance to take control of me. The drug wet is an upper and at times it can make you feel like Superman. Maybe it was a bad idea for me to blow one considering I was already on one hundred. I stuck my head out the door to feel the cool breeze. I peeped a white guy named Teddy who owed me money dip inside the office of the motel. Teddy worked 3rd shift at the front desk of the motel. He would smoke anything he could get his hands on. He reminded me of Jackie Gleason from The Honeymooners and always wore a dull frown. I eased up to the side door that leads to the main office. I pulled my black hoodie over my head and knocked on the door. I saw Teddy in there moving around and if he saw me he wouldn't let me in. I was told I was banned from the motel. I knocked on the door and laid out on the ground pretending, I was sick.

"Hey you can't be out in front like that," he yelled from behind the closed door.

I continued to groan in discomforted with my back facing him. One thing I knew how to do was act. I began to shake violently like I was having a seizure.

"Hey. Hey. You okay?" he called out.

Bingo. I got him. He opened the door.

In a flash, I sprang to my feet and shoved fat boy back into the office. He had a look of horror on his face. I quickly kick the door shut and pulled down the shade. The room was dark, but you could see light pouring out from the other room. I pulled off my dark hoodie and revealed who I was.

"You got my money you owe," I growled.

"I-I uh, was looking for you two days ago," he lied easily.

I leaned in and hit him with a short jab to the middle section. He doubled over clutching his stomach gasping for air. I was sick and tired of people trying to play me. When you're nice to people, people think they can walk all over you. But when I'm forced to play Billy badass people fall in line.

"Go get my money," I told him.

"All I have is twenty-five bucks," he replied handing me the money.

I smacked the money out of his hands. "Do what you been doing go borrow the money out the cash register."

"I can't the boss is on to me."

I leaned again ready to strike.

"Okay. Okay, dammit. I'll get you the money.

I paid close attention as he trudged awkwardly toward the room with the light. He came back and handed me the money. I counted it. "You gave me 50 dollars too much."

"That's for your troubles," he replied.

I took what was owed and let what wasn't fall to the floor. I only wanted what was due to me. I turned on my heels and walked out the door. I didn't know where I was going or what my next move was. For the first time in a long time I had lost my way, and I could feel the jaws of death were closing in.

DAMN

With no place to go, I didn't know who was looking for me or whom I could trust. I found myself back at Gail's place. This time I wasn't sleeping on the couch. I was back in full power with dope and money. So that meant whatever I said goes. A week had passed and the talk all over town was New York had got robbed and shot at by some mask men. I shook my head in disgust, because black people never could get the facts straight enough to save their own lives.

I was on a high alert and didn't leave the house much. To be honest, I was paranoid out of my mind. Every time I heard a police siren or footsteps running up the stairs my antenna went up. It was time for me to move around and put the little Steel City in the rear view mirror.

I bought a '72 Cutlass Supreme in mint condition from an old man who gave it to me for a sweet deal. I had no business buying a car, but I couldn't resist it. I always wanted an old school Cutlass and I absolutely loved it. It was blue with white stripes and the original Cutlass rims. The engine growled like a beast. I had made up my mind I was leaving and heading to Philly as soon as possible. I had a few loose ends to tie up, and then I was going to be on the road. The very next night Gail and I were at a gas station filling up my tank. My plan was to leave at 3 am and never look back.

After I finished pumping my gas, a caravan of unmarked cars and police sirens swooped down on me from every side. “Get your hands up and get on the ground now!”

Everything blurred. Suddenly I was burning inside and the fire was real, exploding to extremity of every nerve on edge, dreading looking at the enormous amount of trouble I was in. I did not resist so I don’t know why the 10 + cops felt the need to rough me up. That’s one of the things I didn’t like about cops. Why treat a suspect like he’s resisting when he’s not? They finally hoisted me up off the ground. A black unmarked car pulled up and the back window rolled down. My eyes couldn’t believe what they were witnessing. I blinked back twice to refocus, sure enough it was New York nodding his head and the car sped off. They stuffed me in the back of a squad car and whisked me off to jail.

I was taken to a small police station and led into an interrogation room. I was bombarded with questions of where I was on the night of the shooting. Of course I said nothing. I didn’t even tell them my name. But when my prints came back, they were jumping up and down with excitement. “Boy we caught a “big fish” out the ocean,” one of the Dicks yelled.

They all gathered around a fax machine and computer, and marveled at my credentials. One of the cops came up to the bars of the holding cell I was in and did a little song and dance, holding my wanted picture up from Illinois. “Hey Mister Big Timer, you’re wanted for armed robbery, you gotta FBI warrant, you got an IDOC warrant...it's niggers like you who should be exterminated," he chuckled.

Instantly rage overwhelmed me and I spit dead in his face. His face turned crimson red and he couldn't get his keys out fast enough to unlock the cage. I got roughed up pretty good. No broken bones but if these PA cops were looking for action then I was the perfect candidate because I refuse to let anyone disrespect me. The very next morning I went in front of a judge who didn't have on the traditional black robe. He wore a pair of jeans and a sweater. I thought that was odd. The courthouse was a small house no bigger than 1000 square feet. Two young women were there to see the judge. They looked at me like I was a monster all shackled up tight. I had shackles around my ankles and cuffs around my wrist a cop on each side.

The judge read the unbelievable charges off. I was being charged with aggravated battery with a firearm, robbery, assault battery, theft, and resisting arrest. I sat there numb listening to the trumped up charges. When it was over there was a white girl in the back room chowing down on a McDonald's Egg McMuffin, waiting to see the judge.

"Hey Chicago wassup?" She whispered.

I studied her face for a split second and immediately I remembered who she was. She was one of the girls from the motel who was strung out on heroin. I used to look out for her and show kindness while the rest of the world was stealing her young innocence.

“Here, I appreciated what you always did for me,” she said handing me an Egg McMuffin sandwich.

I thanked her and tore into the sandwich like it was steak. Minutes later, I was being transported to the Allegheny County Jail. The jail was located on Second Avenue next to the Allegheny River. When I arrived, they placed me in a holding cell and left me there for hours. I think the officer from the other jail I spit on had something to do with me being unfairly treated.

It was after midnight when they finally came to process me into their county jail. I was cold and hungry so I ask to speak to a white shirt. A short middle aged, white man with a barrel of chest came and opened my door.

“Excuse me Lieutenant, I’ve been here since this afternoon and I had not had a phone call or nothing to eat.”

One of the officers pulled him to the side and whispered in his ear. The Lieutenant appeared to be in deep thought. Then he looked over at me, and frowned. “I heard you are a troublemaker and we don’t tolerate nonsense in our jail.”

I shook my head because I knew where this was headed. I was quickly learning, when incarcerated, you were in a no win situation. These people can and will do whatever they wanted to you.

“Alright if you’re not going to do anything close my door,” I smirked.

“What, you’re going to kill yourself?”

“What are you talking about? I didn’t say about killing myself.
“Step back and take your clothes off,” he demanded.

I didn’t know what the hell was going on but there was no way I was taking off my clothes. The room temperature felt like it was below zero in here. If I take off my clothes they were going to have me on suicide watch. When on suicide watch they give you a paper gown to put on and they watch you like a lab rat.

I did not comply. So after a brief standoff they forced me into compliance. I gave them hell for 3 day and 3 nights. I was hilarious; I talked about everyone I could. This beefy officer who looked like he was on steroids was my favorite target. I talked about him so bad all the other officers laughed at him. It wasn’t no secret he didn’t like me and feelings were mutual.

They went out of their way to make my stay as unpleasant as possible by putting me in a mental Pod where there was nothing but loony tune characters running around. I couldn’t believe they had me in a nut house. I wasn't on any meds and I was allowed to come out my cell for a shower and 1 hour of rec time. The doctor told me if I could show behavior improvement, he would send me to general population with the regular offenders. I was literary living in hell and there wasn't a damn thing I could do about it.

BROKEN

I was on my best behavior so I could get out of the crazy Pod. Every day there was some sort of drama, and if you were not crazy hanging around here you soon would be. I kept to myself for the most part. They started giving me a little more time out of my cell. It gave me a chance to breathe. They had a track you could walk around and a porch where you could see the outside world or play basketball. On this particular day, I was out on the track trying to clear my head, when I look up this brown-skinned brother put his hand in my face. I couldn't believe the man had feces on his hand. Immediately I snapped, crackled, and popped. The next thing I knew, I was on top of him pounding my fist into his head and face. I had lost all of my privileges and now I was back at square one. I couldn't win for losing. the story of my life.

Every night in this hell-hole, I heard screams or inmates being dragged out of their cell with feces smeared all over their bodies. This place wasn't designed for peace. In this dark insane world you had to fight to keep your sanity. I was tired and broken; it was hard trying to be strong like an unruffled stone in a storm.

Later that night, I lay awake measuring the great trouble I was in. I turned on the light and splashed cold water on my face. I gazed into the small mirror above the sink. In the mirror stood a man I no longer recognized staring back at me. I was horrified. His eyes had dark ring circles like a raccoon. His skin tone was a shade darker. His face was lean and haggard. Who was this man? *A small voice came from out of nowhere. He is you.*

Tears began to leak out my eyelids. I couldn't stop them even if I wanted to. A loud cry of anguish escaped from somewhere deep in my soul. I felt weak and no longer could stand; my legs gave out from underneath me. I sobbed loudly, shaking, curled up in a fetus position on the cold floor. I cried out to my Lord, my God to take this pain and give me strength to keep fighting on.

I knew the road ahead of me was going to be the toughest challenge of my life. I was twenty-eight years old and I wasn't ready to give up yet. At that moment, I revisited a time when I went to my Pastor Rev. Kenneth Davis to seek some financial help. There was a woman in the church prophesying and she was touching people's forehead. I could feel her powerful energy moving around the room. She was asking people to come down to the Alter. Of course I wasn't going down there and neither did my boy, Jay Fitzpatrick.

However, we sat back and paid attention. Then out of nowhere she called all the men down to the Alter. Grudgingly, we went down and formed a half circle. She began speaking in tongues touching all the men foreheads. When she touched mine she stopped and said, "God has something for you. don't give up on him."

I was spooked, out of all the men in the church I was the only one she delivered a message too. That day had always haunted me and I guess I've been running ever since. It was time for me to stop running and show the world that there is a God that loves me unconditionally. As the sun peeked in my tiny cell window, I did what I always did in time of need. I got on my knees and began to pray, with all I had asking God for His Mercy and Forgiveness. That night marked a new beginning for me. I was grateful for God's warm embrace I felt surrounding me. I knew that troubled waters were ahead, and whatever happens to me God has the final say.

Thirty days later, I had finally made it out to population. I had signed over the title of the Cutlass to Gail. She sold it for a $7,500.00. I know if I was out I could've had gotten at least ten grand. But I couldn't complain. She could've ran off and left me dry. I hired an attorney named R. Goldstein. I explained my situation and he agreed to take on my case. When Gail dropped the money off, he came to see me. The guy was a short mild white guy in his late thirties. He had just started his law firm and he was eager to jump right on the case. I liked how he spoke; he was right to the point. I gave him all the details. He felt the Commonwealth had a weak case, so we were asking for a speedy trial. That meant The Commonwealth of Pennsylvania had 6 months to get their case ready or else I was going to walk.

Being in population meant you had a little more freedom to roam around. They had a gym and a dayroom where you could watch TV, play cards, or chess. Allegheny County Jail was something else. Drugs were everywhere. I saw guy's openly smoking weed and doing cocaine and heroin. That life for me was over with. I never understood why people come to jail and still do drugs in jail. I got deep into the Word; studying it every day.

I became the hoop star on the deck when I got my wind back. I destroyed everybody on the basketball court. I was from Chicago so everyone assumed I could ball. They were right! I put on shows even the COs started taking a liking to me. I began receiving favorable treatment because of my basketball talents, extra food, cigarettes or staying out of my cell late. Nobody wants to be locked in a cell if they don't have to be. I was a long way from home. If I was going to make it; I had to do whatever it took to survive. This was a world like no other and if you were going to make it you had to be strong.

My contemplation on life and being a man taught me that he who cannot change the very fabric of his thought will never be able change his reality, therefore no progress would be made. I had to change everything about me, no more thinking about getting over. No more taking shortcuts or the easy way, because in the end you won't appreciate the journey. I knew I had to reach down deep and pull out that other person on the inside. Who was greater than me, who worked harder than me, who was more dedicated than me? I had to break this old self before it destroyed me and I couldn't do it alone. I needed God to break me down and rebuild me.

During this time in my life God started revealing things and letting me know He was right there. I believe He allows pain to provide healing to make us whole again. I had a lot to learn because doing it my way wasn't working. So I made up my mind and from now on I was going to do it His way. Whatever it took I was willing to put in the work and become a new creation through Christ.

When I Think of Jesus

When I think of Jesus, my face starts to shine like the morning Sun.

Tears begin to mount up in the corner of my eyes.

Then a broad smile appears.

A smile of gratitude.

A smile of gratefulness to my Lord and Savior Jesus Christ.

Who died for me.

When I think of Jesus, I think of God. Who truly was Jesus.

The words He spoke.

The truth He taught.

With the lives He saved.

Hallelujah! For Jesus he's alive in me.

So when I think of Jesus

I think of pure Love.

CAN'T NOBODY HOLD ME DOWN

Months had flown by and I was getting stronger mentally, physically, and spiritually. My attorney was putting things together and things were looking up. Although I terribly missed my family, there was nothing I could do but pray for them each and every day. I hadn't had a cellmate in a week and I was hoping when I got a new one he wouldn't be unclean. One thing I hated about being locked up was having an unclean cellmate. If they didn't take care of the cell, I didn't care how big they were or how tough they were we were going to fight.

The very day I received a new cellmate and I couldn't believe my eyes. It was the black guy who was spending all that money with me at the motel. His name was Anthony and right away we did some catching up. Again God was amazing. He was showing me things that were leaving me speechless. Anthony knew the Bible inside and out that was a blessing because we fellowshipped a lot.

One thing about Anthony he always wore a huge smile like sunshine and his face glowed. He walked in the light and I knew God sent him to me. The signs were adding up and I was paying attention. The night I met Anthony he told me he slipped out of a preacher's house that he was living with in a drug program. Anthony was good with his hands he was a contractor. The preacher sold his own Mercedes Benz and purchased Anthony a brand new truck for his business. He said things were going so good he wanted to celebrate and that's when he ran into me.

Anthony wanted to get into another drug program to avoid going to prison. So I wrote a letter on his behalf and 3 weeks later he was accepted into the program. I was happy for him and I wished him well. My trial date was coming up and I was ready to get it over with. But I had received some disturbing news from back home. Du Page County wanted to do a photo line-up of me in Pittsburg.

They were trying to put an armed robbery on me that I had nothing to with. I did my fair share of dirt but that I didn't have any part of. The lady who got robbed now works in Pittsburgh. I was flabbergasted. I couldn't believe what they were trying to do. They were trying to stack the deck against me back home because they didn't have enough evidence to nail me. So they were trying to pen anything on me. I took to prayer and gave it to God.

A month later, I was being lead into a small room with five other guys who looked nothing like me. Du Page was paying each one of them twenty dollars to participate in the photo line-up. I was not a happy camper and I expressed my disappointment to my attorney when he arrived. He walked into the room and was pissed. He told all the parties that were involved, "If it's not right for my brother; it's not right for my client. If I have to go from pod to pod to find five guys who look like my client that's what I'm willing to do." Then he started quoting statues of the law. They ended up postponing the line-up. I was relieved and very appreciative of what my attorney did for me. I didn't have any more money to pay him, and for him to do that from the kindness of his heart that was all love.

One week later I received a letter from my attorney stating, "Dear Mr. Harris you no longer have to worry about that photo line-up, the witness refused to testify." Wow! Don't tell me prayer doesn't work. Again God was showing me He was right there.

On the morning of my trial I got up and felt at ease. I read a couple of scriptures and got dressed. On my way to the courthouse, I heard a loud car stereo bumping Puffy Daddy's, *Can't Nobody Hold Me Down*. I nodded my head because at that moment that's exactly how I felt. No matter what you go through don't let nobody hold you down.

I held my head up, as I was being lead in shackles inside of the courthouse. We were all cramped into a large holding cell that held about seventy-five people. I was facing 5 to 10 years in a Pennsylvania Prison if convicted. While going to court you were allowed to wear your street clothes. Back home that wasn't possible. I guess they feared someone would escape. My attorney finally came down to get me and we went upstairs to the courtroom. The courtroom was empty, just the prosecutor and a court reporter. I sat down in a chair behind the defendant table. My nerves were on edge.

I felt like fresh meat being placed in a frying pan waiting for the burner to come on.

Court was a scary place especially when your life was hanging in the balance. I sat there for a good thirty minutes until the judge called all parties to his chambers. I didn't know what was going on, but there we were sitting in the judge's chamber. He sat behind a large mahogany colored desk with his hands folded across his bulging mid-section. The prosecutor was asking for more time. He stressed the witness couldn't be found. The judge listened intently as he stood up from his chair. He was an aging, short white man with gray hair. Every now and then his gaze fell on me, and then he would look away.

"Look, I have reviewed this case and let me tell you, it stinks. You had 6 months to prepare for this case. If your witness is not here by noon then I have no choice, but to dismiss count 1 of aggravated battery of a firearm. You have no firearm. You have no witness. Geeeesh! I have other things I could be doing. You have until noon," the judge told him turning back b his newspaper.

My attorney walked me back down to the holding cell. I had mixed emotions; I wanted this case over with. I was tired and ready to go home. I paced back and forth waiting and waiting. Hours had passed. I looked up and it was 3 o'clock. My attorney came down and said he was working out a deal that would not require jail time. Moments later I was taken back up to the courtroom. I copped out to

18-month probation for simple robbery and stolen property. I was being accused of robbing the motel and stealing my own property back. I didn't agree with the charges but at the end of the day I was pleased the gun case was thrown out. I thanked my attorney for a job well done. I just wanted to get as far away from Pittsburgh as possible. I had no ill feeling about the "Burg" I met some wonderful people I will never forget. But it was time for me to return home and face the music.

On the ride back to the jail I had a huge Kool-Aid smile plastered all over my face. For the first time in a long time I felt like the weight of the world was off my chest. I glanced out the window enjoying the sight-seeing as the van rolled through downtown Pittsburgh. When you're locked down, you would gravitate towards anything that wasn't jailhouse related. The van pulled up next to a car at a red light. The car's stereo was turned up loud. My Kool-Aid smile just got bigger as I sang in unison. *CAN'T NOBODY HOLD ME DOWN OHH NO I GOT TO KEEP ON MOVINNNNNN.'*

DON'T WORRY BE HAPPY

When I got back to the jail they immediately moved me to another part of the jail. This Pod held fugitives, federal prisoners and juvenile offenders. When I saw kids who were as young as 15 years old locked up with grown men I was astonished. They had their own cellblock downstairs, but damn they were still locked up and interacting with grown men. I was a bit concerned because I never saw anything like this back home. I went upstairs to my assigned cell and admired the view of the Allegheny River.

Lately TV reporters had been swarming the jail because a high profile murder took place. An informant was schedule to testify against a Drug Kingpin, but somehow he was found with a needle in his arm in PC (Protective Custody). It doesn't take a rocket scientist to figure out what happened to him; considering the Police were the only ones who had keys to his cell. I was learning in a heartbeat jail was hell on earth.

I went to the open porch and got some shots up on the basketball court. It didn't take long for the kids to come out and see who was the new guy out there scorching the nets. Right away they took a liking to me. I met a 17-year-old from Elgin Illinois he was charged with attempted murder. Elgin was 25 minutes away from Aurora where I lived. Indeed, the world was small. I didn't know how I was going to do it, but I knew God wanted me to do something.

The next day after breakfast, I went into a small room on the Pod where mostly bible studies were held at. Each Pod in the jail had one. Two younger brothers were in there studying The Word. I introduced myself and joined them. It was at that moment when I knew what God wanted me to do.

My time was running out in Pittsburgh. The State of Illinois had another week to extradite me back home. Every day, I try to reach out to the kids and showed them there is someone greater than them. I used basketball as a tool to reach them. Some gravitated towards me others did not. Every day I held fellowship with these young brothers not just to talk about the Bible but about life too.

These kids were amazing and I had to let them know how valuable their self-worth and self-love was. I went from having two kids to more than twenty kids. When I looked up the room was packed. Black and brown kids staring back at me with wide eyes. Some of them sitting here at first rejected me, now they looked forward to our fellowship meeting every day.

God is good and at this time in my life even though I was locked under key, I was content and wasn't worried about anything including the drama that was waiting for me back home. The next day we were having a great fellowship meeting. There was plenty of laughter and great conversation. Then this kid named X had finally walked into our meeting. X was a 16-year-old black kid who spent most of his time clowning others. He was mad funny; I will give him that. But this kid had so much talent it was crazy. Whatever he did he was good at - art, basketball, and chess.

Xavier was very well spoken for a boy of his age. The whole time I was there he resisted me. So last night I told him whatever he was going through God will go through it with him. When he walked in we all stood up and gave him some love. This time we clowned him, for taking so long to join us.

We were getting ready to close our meeting in prayer when there was a knock on the door. My time had come I had to go back home to Illinois. As long as I live, I will never forget the heartfelt prayer this kid sent me off with. Tears stun my eyes and even as I write today tears are still there. Each one of them expressed their gratitude and like I told them it was all love. The glory goes to God and when you come from under this rock make sure you make Him proud.

I went to my cell and grabbed all my belongings. Everything I had I gave to those kids; food, cloths, pens, writing pads and some of my best poetry. I like to think I gave them some inspiration to do better. We all fall short of God's glory. It took a while for me to finally get out the door. Even the C. O's wished me well.

When I got downstairs two white men with chains and shackles were waiting for me, they watched me like a hawk as I was allowed to put back on my street clothes. The booking officer was having a hard time identifying me. When you are being processed into the jail, they take your picture and give you a wristband as your ID. On that wristband is your picture with your government name and a number. My picture didn't look like me so they refused to hand me over to the Extradition Transporters. I must admit the photo looked nothing like me. I was now a new creation the old me was dead. The new me was alive and well.

The captain of the Allegheny County jail had come down and took a look at my picture he too said it wasn't me. He ordered them to retake my fingerprints. We all waited patiently and when my prints came back a positive match they were left shaking their heads.

"Wow, if I was a betting man, I would've lost this bet," the captain said.

After waiting for more than an hour I was chained, shackled and stuffed into a small white van with three other prisoners. I hated riding in close confinement vehicles with little air to breathe. But it wasn't about what I hated it's was more about what I was putting myself through. No one told me to become an outlaw. If a man can make his bed he should have no problem laying in it. The van pulled out of Allegheny County Jail and a cool sense of relief sweep over me. I had dodged a huge bullet and I can't lie, I only hoped I could dodge another one when I got home.

I'M READY

The ride home was nothing nice. The first 5 hours of the ride had my long legs cramping up. Along the route, we picked up three more prisoners. We were really packed in there like sardines. One of the prisoners was a young Mexican woman who was being transported to the Kane County Jail. We both were headed to the same destination. She was from Elgin, Illinois. The van had come to a stop and we were all put on a bus that sort of looked like a Greyhound bus.

It felt cozy and all the officers were black. They had a TV and they also played nothing but soulful music. But being cuffed to a stranger that probably had not showered in a week, I could've done without.

I was on two different buses for 3 days as we made our way to Nashville, Tennessee. Nashville was the home base of the Expedite Transportation Center. Here they put all the detainees in 4 large holding cells. Whatever state you were wanted in you had to get on a certain bus. For example, if you were going to California you would be placed on the West Coast Bus. I was headed to Illinois so I was placed on Bus # 2 the Midwest. Twelve hours later, I had finally arrived at Kane County Jail. I was home and ready to do battle.

It didn't take long for them to get me in front of a judge. The judge read 4 counts of armed robbery. Each count carried 6 to 30 years. I was facing life in prison if convicted. On the same day, I was also transported to Du Page County Court House where I was facing 2 counts of armed robbery there. To sum it up, I was in a whole heap of trouble. I wasn't too worried about Kane County, I was guilty there and as a man I was willing to take my punishment. But Du Page put 2 counts of armed robbery on me that I had nothing to do with and I resented them for that.

Three weeks later I was transported up North to McHenry County Jail due to overcrowding in the Kane County Jail. McHenry County Jail was a lot better than Kane County. Food was better and the jail was cleaner. I tried my best to keep to myself but the devil always knew what buttons to push. One day I was in the day room reading The Chicago Sun Times newspaper, something I did every morning before I worked out. A Chinese guy kept walking around the table giving me dirty looks. So I asked him do we have a problem.

The short little guy told me to get up and started charging at me like he was a Bull. They were five Chinese guys on the deck and when one fights they all fight. They wore green uniforms because they were federal prisoners and the jail was getting big money for housing federal prisoners.

Immediately, I jumped on my feet and hit the little charging Chinese Bull with a hard straight right to the head. He stumbled backward, collapsed, and didn't move again. Next four Chinese guys bum rushed me and started throwing fist and flying kicks. This was a bad Chinese movie because it didn't end well for them. When you're being attacked you have no choice but to fight back and fighting back is what I did. I was landing clean shots sending them plummeting to the floor.

Moments later, C. O's flooded the cellblock spraying huge cans of orange mace. Everybody ran for cover because being maced wasn't no joke. Once mace hit your eyes it left you irritated and disoriented.

It didn't take long for the good ole boys to come and put handcuffs on me. I'm quite sure the Good Samaritan inmates were very helpful. Even though I didn't need any help, it was sad to see no one came to my aid but my cellmate K-Folks Graves. That's one thing I dislike about my black brothers. We don't stick together not even in the belly of the beast. Every other race sticks together Whites, Hispanics, and Asians. Blacks are the only tribe who is lost in the wilderness. Instead of depending on our dominance and our strength in numbers, we sell out to the powers that be for a little of nothing. The more I saw who we were as black men the more I was disappointed.

I was taking to the hole; a place I was starting to get familiar with. I didn't mind going to the hole for a good cause. But to see nothing happen to the Chinese men left a sour taste in my mouth. I was the one who was assaulted and jumped by 5 guys. I was finding out in a hurry that even in jail a black man didn't have a leg to stand on.

At my hearing, two officers read me my charges and they informed me that every witness said I started the fight.

"What do you mean I started the fight?" I said angrily.

"Look we got 3 witnesses that say you started the incident," the officer stated.

"You guys got cameras. Look at the cameras and you will see," I pleaded.

Apparently they weren't trying to hear me, because they booked me for 30 days in the hole. I took the grain along with the salt and kept it moving. Again I couldn't win for losing my new nickname was the Chinese Assassin.

For months I traveled back and forth to Kane County and Du Page County courthouses. The see-saw trip was just too aggravating to deal with. Because I was up North in McHenry, the ride in a back of a paddy wagon is nothing nice for an hour and half drive. I could never breathe in those meat wagons. I filed a motion to stay in Du Page County and my motion was granted in August of 2000.

In one year, I had visited four county jails and Du Page County was the worse of them all. When I say white people had privileges, man they had privileges! They had the best jobs and if they wanted you out of a cellblock they will go behind your back, and collect signatures and give it to the police. Countless numbers of times I saw white male child molesters get a slap on the wrist sentence. While blacks get slammed for a crack cocaine possession I was getting an up close lesson on how corrupt and unjust the system was. If you were black or brown you better hop on the first good deal you saw leaving the station. If not you're going to wish you had.

In March of 2001, it was time for me to go to trial. For the record, Du Page County never offered me a sweet deal I could not refuse. So I had no choice but to take them the full 15 rounds. I was considered a heavy weight that they did not like. I had already locked a deal with Kane County. I would plead guilty for exchange of a 10-year sentence. That was fair and I willing to take ownership of the crime. But in Du Page, they were sticking one of the crimes on me I had nothing to do with. I did not match the robber's height, weight or ammo. But Du Page didn't care they were looking to solve cases. What you see on Law and Order, where the prosecutor goes beyond the call of duty to find the right perpetrator who committed the crime, doesn't exist in the real world.

Months before my trial, I was visited by detectives who were still trying to get me to confess to crimes I had nothing to do with. These were the same detectives who came to see me in McHenry County. They wanted me to help myself, meaning if I knew of any other crimes like unsolved murders or high rolling drug dealers. I told them what I told them last time "Good day gentleman," and called for the guard to take me back to my cell. Talking to the police was something you didn't do. However, before I left they praised me for being a smart man. But they told me they were prepared to do whatever it took to secure a conviction on me.

The day before trial my attorney came to see me. She had an upbeat look on her face. I asked her a mind full of questions. I'm not going to lie I was more nervous than a turkey going into a slaughterhouse. Every motion we put in we lost. We even lost the motion to show proof the mask they had didn't have any DNA to match me. This alone will prove my innocence. They had a gun that's not mine nor was it used in the crime, but they were allowed to use it in evidence. I was pissed and the more she talked the more I knew I was doomed.

That night I couldn't sleep. I paced the tiny 5 by 10 box all night. The devil was on my shoulder and I couldn't shake him off. *Where is your God now? Tomorrow they're going to hang you.* I sat down on my bunk and tried by best to block out the noise. I reviewed my notes for tomorrow and closed my eyes. My mind was fatigued and my body felt drained. No doubt tomorrow was going to be the biggest day of my life. *God, do not forsake me.*

LYFE

The next morning, I woke up and did 200 push-ups. Everyone on the deck knew today was my day. I showered and did not eat anything. I got dressed in the orange jump suit that read Du page County Jail. Every Prison or County Jail in this country has a label to mark their free meal ticket. We were worth money and lots of it. I felt like a fool being caught up into the trap. These people control everything, what you see, what you eat, what you hear.

This was the third time I was going to be sitting in the defendant chair and so far I was batting a thousand. The C.O. buzzed my cell door and it was time for me to make that walk. I had a bad feeling rising in my chest. I tried my best to suppress it but the premonition wouldn't dissolve. As I was leaving the cellblock other inmates wished me luck. I made the long dreaded walk down the hall to the elevator. The C.O. made small talk trying to loosen me up. I thanked him and made my way towards the courtroom.

They moved me toward the courtroom where my trial was being held. I changed into a gray suit with a crisp white button up and a pair of black shoes. I looked dapper and a suit still looked good on me. I was sitting in a holding cell when a Guard asked me to step out so an inmate could use the bathroom. When the inmate came up the stairs and walked right past me, black rage smothered my thoughts. My face tightened, and my fist, were clenched. The white guy who betrayed me held his head down like the snake he was and walked right past me. He was here to testify against me. Without his testimony the state had no case. I couldn't believe this guy sold me out on a lie for a crime he knows I didn't commit. My first reaction was to smash his head in. But I was rockin' with Jesus. I was a new creation so I had to eat my anger.

The courtroom was packed and the prosecution team of Laurel and Hardy wasted no time telling the jury how much of a bad guy I was. They made it seem as if I was the John Gotti of armed robberies. I sat in disgust with a pen in my hand taking notes. I know what I did and what I did not do. It was hard listening to lies that were fabricated to paint their picture. They made it seem like we were doing robberies for drugs. I had over 60 grand and could have bought all the drugs I wanted if that were the case. But they had to establish a motive in order to fit their agenda. Even if it were a lie their job was to sell fake news to the jury.

For hours they brought bogus witnesses and allowed evidence that had nothing to do with me. I was heated and I let my attorney have it at intermission.

"Whose team you on?" I spat angrily.

"I'm on your team," She replied running a hand through her short crop blonde hair.

"Well act like it and go after them."

The fix was in and I felt like she wasn't doing enough. The prosecution team could do no wrong and the judge granted them everything they asked for. If they would've, asked for my arm she would've given it to them. I needed my Attorney to work for me, if not I was going down in flames.

Court was back in session and the on slaughter continued. This went on for hours until both sides rested their cases. It took the jury two hours to reach a verdict. They escorted me back into the courtroom and to be honest I knew I was in trouble. There was only one black on the panel and he was far from my peer. He looked at me with guilty eyes so I knew he couldn't help me. All three witnesses first written statements did not finger me as the suspect. But when they took the stand they all had new statements identifying me as the suspect.

I was hoping the jury would see through the pack of lies. Du Page County conviction rate was at a remarkable 98% so the odds were definitely not in my favor. When the jury filed into the courtroom, I tried to read their body language. They say body language speaks volumes if this is true my outcome was not promising. Each one of them had a grim look on their face. The judge walked in and everybody stood up. Her face was pale and her expression was stone-like. I didn't know what to expect. I felt like a bird on a wire.

"Has the jury reached a verdict?" the judge inquired.

"Yes your Honor."

"Will the defendant rise?"

"We the jury find the defendant Jerald Harris, guilty."

Guilty? I said inwardly in disbelief. *How? Their whole case was built on the testimony of a crackhead who lied to get a favorable deal to save himself. He gave numerous of inconsistent statements. You idiots can't see through this bullshit." I wanted to scream. God I couldn't believe this! I was panicking inside, because a guilty verdict meant I was going away on a long vacation and not by choice.*

I was starting to realize you never fully understand a situation until your feet are the one being held over the fire. Anger was an understatement. I was burning hot coals of lava within. And just when I thought I was free on the inside, those old festering demons were beginning to resurface. The man I was trying to run away from was suddenly back knocking on my door.

Remarkably, I somehow managed to keep my outer being in check long enough for them to usher me out of the courtroom. Trust and believe it wasn't easy, because I wanted to wild out.

Tears stung the corner of my eye slits, but I refuse to let them fall. I wouldn't give these bastards the satisfaction of seeing me break down like some old car on the freeway. However, as I was leaving the courtroom everything seemed to move in slow motion. The judge's cold eyes spoke volumes. This was just another day at the office for her. She was so much of a coward she couldn't look me in the eyes. The prosecution team gave each other high fives and pats on the back. If this was a championship game indeed they had just won the trophy.

The world that I once knew was gone and it wasn't a damn thing I could do about it. All I kept thinking about was my seven-year-old son. I had failed him. If I could somehow make my life disappear this would've been a good time. Deep down I felt the storm coming; those cops said they were going to do whatever to get a conviction with or without my cooperation. I didn't sell my soul; however, I played the game and lost. The song Life, by K.C & Jo-Jo began to sing loudly in my ear. The song just wouldn't go away. It just wouldn't.

THE DEFENDANT CHAIR

The arguments were over and the black robe takes a seat.

The Jury comes back into the courtroom my knees became instantly weak.

The Media is in a frenzy and they make a nice penny of someone else's misery.

I see too many suits and ties.

I see too much corruption in one room real eyes recognize.

The world spits you out, tosses you up, flips you over and gives it to you raw.

Game over.

See, I can't keep fighting a fight that has no fear.

I have to stand clear in mind and pure in desire

And never again late temptations light my fire.

The Defendant chair is cold, got my soul on hold

A black man caught up in the system, for them it's a pot of gold.

Eyes must stay woke ain't got time for no sleeping

The devil in the black robe mission is clear

destroy God's people.

GUILTY! GUILTY! GUILTY!

Truth can't come from lying lips, too many tricks

Looks like I'm headed on a long trip.

Lessons learned, ego's crushed, pistols bursting in air

Never again I swear will I sit in the Defendant Chair.

ONLY GOD CAN JUDGE ME

Weeks have gone by and my sentence day was quickly approaching. I was facing a maximum of 6 to 30 years on each count by law they could give me 90 years. I was prepared to use the case *Apprendi v. New Jersey.* I had been studying case law in the Du Page County Library. I wasn't going to keep relying on my ineffective counsel.

According to the Law they had to sentence me under the state guidelines. I wasn't a career criminal, so they couldn't give me the maximum. I was on pins and needles stressing because I felt like my soul was on ice. The worst thing in the world is to be stuck in limbo. I stayed in prayer; kept praising God no matter how many times the enemy tried to intervene. I stayed solid as a rock. I know God didn't bring be this far to fail me.

On the morning of my sentence I felt good as I was ushered into the courtroom. Wow! The courtroom was packed. I saw my mother and my younger sister and my baby niece seated in the front row behind me. I saw a few other familiar faces; lying cops, a couple female friends, and a host of newspaper reporters. There was a chill in the air that made the tiny hair on my forearms stand up. My life was on the line and I had a judge that was known to hang black and brown people.

It didn't take long for the prosecution team to start shooting daggers in my directions. According to them I was the worst scumbag on earth. What they failed to mention was, I didn't hurt anyone, or I didn't kill anyone. There's no doubt I should get punished but to hang an extra case on me I did not do, I still had a problem with that. To find me guilty for a crime and have the evidence that could exonerate me, but choose to ignore it instead. Boy! I was still smokin.'

My due process rights were clearly being violated. One thing I learned the system never plays fair. The weak and the poor suffer the most while the rich give money to go unscathed. When things don't add up that's when you have to pay attention. The game is cold but it's fair. To every game played there are rules and regulations you must follow. If you don't abide by the rules you can't compete at a higher level in the game. *Know somthin' before you do somthin.'*

The state was wrapping up their closing argument and my mouth fell open when they asked the judge to sentence me to 60 years in prison. There was a sharp cry that escaped my mother's mouth. It was obvious these people hated my guts. I handed my attorney a paper. On it was a copy of the Apprendi v New Jersey case law. She looked at me puzzled then a sly grin cracked her thin lips.

"Nice this may come in handy," she winked.

I refused to just let these people do anything to me. I sat back long enough and realized no one cares more about you then yourself. Self-love and self-worth means so much because when you love yourself, you value your life. Gems were coming at me and I was starting to gather a small treasure. Words had the ability to breathe life into you and the more I fed my brain, the hungrier I became.

When it was time for me to speak I didn't have the slightest idea of what I was going to say. So there I was the big bad wolf standing face to face with the judge who held my life in her hands.

"Your Honor I have been coming to your courtroom for over 18 months. I have always been respectable and I have always looked you in the eye. With all due respect your Honor you have not been fair. Every motion we have filed you have denied, even evidence that could prove without a doubt I did not commit the crime you denied. Your Honor the system stinks not because of its laws. Its stinks because the people we put in place abuses the law for their purpose. You can't pick and choose who you like or don't like. The prosecutor seems to think I should serve 60 years for a crime that carries no more than 30. He's the same man who gave a 28-year-old white man who repeatedly raped his neighbor's 11 year old daughter 6 years. Is justice blind? Don't let my black skin stop you from being fair. Deep down we all are the same and we come from the same place. To be truthful only God can judge me and what you decide to sentence me God allowed."

The judge leaned back in her chair. I guess to gather her thoughts. She began by giving me a short history lesson on who she was and what she stood for. No matter what she claimed her actions told her story. I was far more intelligent than I looked so her brief rebuttal didn't move me. When she finished she turned towards me and paused.

"Mr. Harris I have no choice not only to protect the public, but also to deter others. I think the state without a doubt proved their case. Therefore, I sentence you to 25 years on count 1, 25 years on count 2, and 25 years on count 3 run concurrent."

25 years??? My insides were screaming my whole world had just collapsed. There's no way I deserved 25 years. I barely had a background. My mother didn't take the news well she collapsed and I felt bad for taking her through this madness. Reporters quickly exited the courtroom everything seemed like a bad nightmare. My attorney was livid as she shook her head in disbelief and mumbled words I could not make out. The bailiff wasted no time getting me out of there. I noticed all eyes were on me as I exited the courtroom. The self-satisfied smirk of the prosecutors face I will never forget.

The walk back to the cellblock was difficult, bad news traveled fast. I heard things like "Keep ya head up J or you will get it back on appeal." Twenty-five years was a hard pill to swallow and the pain in my chest was heavy. They sent a psych doctor and a nurse to make sure I wasn't going to hurt myself. I told them I was fine and went to my cell and locked up. I just wanted to be left alone I didn't want anyone's sympathy. I made this bed and I had no choice but to lay in it. I opened my Bible and quickly closed it; the last thing I wanted to do was read. The devil was back and he was in my head. *Where is your God now? Who's going look after those kids? You can't trust what you can't see.* I was being flooded with unwanted thoughts. This by far is going to be the toughest challenge of my life.

One month later I was back in the Big House (Joliet Correctional Center.) God I couldn't believe I was back in the house of hell. This time I knew what to expect I guess you can say I was seasoned. A man from the staff interviewed me and when I told them I had 25 years. Instantly his facial expression changed.

"You got 25 years for an armed robbery? That's pretty excessive. You're not a career criminal. Wow they screwed you over. Good luck," the man said.

I was used to people sharing their opinion, but I could care less about what they thought. I was the one who had to do the time. I had to do twelve and a half years. That means I wasn't guaranteed to make it. One thing about prison anything could happen at any time. Anything over 25 years was considered life. Everything seemed surreal. I had to ask myself was this really happening to me. I was feeling some kind of way and my spirit was down. My celly was an older man; we called him "Pops." Pops didn't bother anyone. He mostly kept to himself. One night after chow he shared with me that he had owed a guy named Low-End fifty dollars for a bag of dope.

I couldn't believe Pop's got out there like that. But then again this was prison. You couldn't trust anything over anybody. Some people were not who they say they were. Drugs were around if you were looking for them. Marijuana, heroin, and cocaine; if you had the money you could get almost anything.

I was coming back from the yard and I could see somebody standing outside my cell. The sheet was up and this guy was telling me his man was in their taking care of some business. Immediately, I put two and two together and I just lost it. I pushed the little swollen guy out of my way and tore down the sheet that hung from the bars. Pop's was performing a sex act. I was disgusted and I couldn't stop my rage that was bubbling over.

A tall thin dark cat with long French braids named Low End quickly pulled up his sweat pants around his hips. "Aye Joe what you on?" He questioned.

I didn't waste any time going in on him. I grabbed a fist full of his long braids and used his face as a punching bag. It was disrespectful to have homosexual relationships where a man laid his head. If Pops wanted to be about that life, there's no way he could live around me. Homosexual activity was forbidden and the ones who indulged I wanted far away from me as possible. What a man does with his own body I could care less but when it came to our cell he will act accordingly or there's going to be a situation. I was already having a hard time dealing with prison and to see so much homosexual activity I was disappointed in my black brothers for being weak. I could never understand why a man would sleep with another man than pretend that he is not gay. To each its own but at the end of the day I call it as I see it.

As for Pops he was an undercover homosexual. He couldn't pay his drug debt so he did what he did best. I am a man's man, strong, confident, and resilient. What my poor eyes had to bear witness to in prison was shocking and unappealing. When a man is incarcerated the first thing he misses besides his love ones is the intimacy from a woman. I struggled with the loss of a woman's touch. Just to smell her hair would be refreshing. I didn't know how I was going to be able to do 12 more years without the warmth of a woman's love.

Some inmates stalked the female officers day and night just to get a glimpse of them, then run back in there cells to choke their chicken. I had a celly that used to go to sick call twice a week to see old white women. Now for sick call they charged you 5 dollars per visit; I guess to deter inmates from stalking their women. Prison is one big sex pool, male officers slept with female officers and inmates slept with, whoever they could. I knew in order to survive what I craved the most I was going to have to get stronger. I prayed for strength each and every day, because the devil kept coming.

ON THE MOVE

Finally, they had me on transfer and as the blue bird bus pulled out of Joliet State Penitentiary, it felt good to be leaving the hotel of hell. My next stop was Shawnee Correctional Center in Vienna, Illinois. Shawnee was six hours away from Chicago. It was 20 minutes away from Kentucky. Other inmates who had been there before had nothing pleasant to say about the place except it didn't snow down there much.

The main concern I had in prison was staying healthy and alive. That was my number one goal. You could easily lose your life in prison; from fighting, gang violations, suicides or even stress. I was in the early stages of my bid and I have already seen so much. A man has to really be strong to hold on to his sanity when he's living in the devil's den.

Ten hours later a bus carrying me, and about 30 more inmates had finally made it to Shawnee. The prison reminded me of Illinois River Correctional Center. We were told to be quiet and listen for our name and prison number. Then we were all led into a receiving area; where we were ordered to strip, bend over, and cough. I don't know how these men could have a job looking up a man's rectum all day. I don't care how much they paid me. There are certain things, a man just don't do.

The worst part about being in prison is having no money. When you don't have the luxuries such as a TV, radio, hot pot, and food your bid will become even more difficult. I've seen grown men do some strange things for some change. Washing another man's underwear or cleaning his cell with a toothbrush; I found that to be self-degrading. A man that values his self-worth would rather starve then eat poison from a tree. When you're in the jungle the worst thing a man could be is a sheep.

After 3 months in Shawnee, I was sent to Dixon Correctional Center on a court writ. Dixon, Illinois was President Ronald Reagan's childhood hometown. The town was small with a population of fifteen thousand. The prison was huge. It was like being in a little city. There were streets with stop signs and there were no bars. Sometimes I felt like I wasn't incarcerated. There was so much to do which helped to keep your mind off of doing time.

Dixon was only an hour away from home and I was doing everything in my power to try and stay there. The Atown family was down here Godfather, Timmy, O'Shea, Dino, Green Eyes, Jody, Chevlle and Sosa. It didn't matter your affiliation; we were Aurora "ATown" it was one love.

The only thing I did not like about being on a court writ was they had you in a bright yellow suit walking around looking like a banana. I was shooting cats out on the basketball court every chance I got. It didn't take long for a guy named Nine-Nine to take notice.

He slipped me a short outfit and a pair of shoes to play on his team. I gladly accepted and couldn't wait to torch the Folks team. This was a hustle if we win each man got 10 dollars.

Nine-Nine was a gambling man and he put up big money. Big money meant a whole lot of commissary. Commissary was a man's paradise behind bars. There was nothing like having your own food, clothing and other luxuries they provide at the canteen. Grown men found themselves acting like little kids in a candy store when it was time to go to commissary.

In my free time, Dixon had an exceptional Law Library and I spent as much time as possible working on my case to get back in court to give them their bogus 25 years back. Of course there were jailhouse attorneys that knew everything. One thing I didn't understand about jailhouse attorneys. If they were so smart, why is it they could never get themselves out of prison?

On September 11, 2001, I was awakened to loud sirens and people, screaming we are under attack. The joint was immediately placed on level one lockdown. We watched from our cells on TV the horrific terrorist attack on the World Trade buildings in New York. Words cannot explain the deepest sorrow I felt for those thousands of innocent people who lost their lives that day. With all the madness going on this was a bad time to be behind bars. You wanted to be out there with your family and loved ones during this time of crisis.

Prison was like being buried alive and you never knew how much air you had left to stay alive. We could hear and see the world but we couldn't touch it.

In November 2001, I was sent back to Shawnee. I copped a plea for 10 years on the Kane County case, to be run concurrent with the twenty-five-year sentence from Du Page County. The twenty-five years will eat up the ten, which means it does not affect my sentence. I was tired of looking at courtrooms after courtrooms. I needed to get settled in so I could focus. I felt like I was living in an old house where everything needed to be fixed all the time.

I had a new celly named Big Face, and he was a character. He was Folks and at times we bumped heads. Prison is so hard, not only do you have to deal with racist C. O's but you also had to have a decent cellmate you could get along with. They were like gems that were hard to find. You had to live with that guy in 5 X 10 box.

Big Face could be cool, but he had a special admiration for men that were trying to be women, they were known as "sissy" boys. That's where we did not see eye to eye. There were plenty of men pretending to be women walking around the joint. I didn't believe in being gay in prison and then when you go back into the world you were no longer gay. AIDS was real in the penitentiary and you had men who looked and acted like women spreading the deadly disease around like cupcakes. I kept my mask on at all times letting them know I didn't play reindeer games.

Shawnee was hell on earth. In the summer, the cells would get so hot the devil would be sitting in the corner smiling. Even the brick walls would sweat. Now I knew how bread felt baking in an oven. Shawnee did have its upside. I met some good brothers there I will forever call friends. Johnny Quick Mitchell who happens to be the brother of Twista, one of Chicago's legendary rappers. Quick was solid a real smooth brother. Dave "Dawud" Bryant and Shawn "Chief" Russell were also a couple of good brothers.

I was learning a lot about myself, learning to love me first. So I started reading anything that would help mold a better me. I was looking for substance. *The Autobiography's of Malcolm X* and *Martin Luther King Jr.* were amazing; both of these great leaders knew they were facing death every time they walked outside their door. It takes a strong man to stand up and die for what he believes in. Those great leaders paid the ultimate price and when I look at black men today, we're killing each other and dying for nothing. I read everything from Gandhi to Adolf Hitler. Reading is something I never did in the free world; books to me were boring, now they were giving me life. I heard the old saying. *If you want to keep information away from the black man put it in a book.*

One night my man, Yogi, had some new books that just came in. I scanned through a few until one caught my eye. The book was called, *A Breed Apart,* written by Victor Woods. Without any hesitation, I knew I had to read this book. Yogi told me to give him 2 noodles, a summer sausage and a chili. I wasn't trying to buy the book all I wanted to do was read it but Yogi was a hustler so I met his demands and the book was mine. Right away I tore into the book and couldn't put it down. Victor Woods was someone I could identify with. This cat had gone to prison and got out and turned his life around. The book was so good I read it twice, just in case I missed something the first time.

In prison, I read hundreds of books that were decent, but *A Breed Apart* caught my attention the most. I starting thinking Victor Wood and I, wasn't too far from being a breed apart. I started seeing him all over television CNN and FOX NEWS. The man was definitely an inspiration. If he can change for the better, so could I. Deep down within, me lived a true writer. I always had a way with words, *maybe one day I could tell my story*. The wheels in my head started turning and the more I thought about it I knew I was going to do everything in my power to make my vision a reality. When I touch down, I was going to look for Mr. Victor Woods and tell him personally what his story did for me.

I started picking back up the pen. I would write deep thoughts and poems. I loved writing poems because poems allowed me to draw deep from the well within. A man will never know what he's capable of if he doesn't give it a try. I was tired of bumping my head up against the stone wall. I had to find my own lane to ride in that didn't involve anything illegal. I had a lot of years left to give these people if I didn't give this time back. I got a letter yesterday that denied my motion for a hearing to reconsider my sentence. The system was definitely unfair. If you lacked resources or help from the outside world you had a slim chance in hell at getting back to court. I tried not to think about time and the outside world because it was evident the outside world wasn't thinking about me, and it hurt.

I had to pick up the pieces and kill my emotions. If I didn't, I was not going to make it out of here with a sane mind. When you're trying to change the devil is always lurking around each corner. The Black Rain never seems to let up it's a pain you have to live.

UNBREAKABLE

You can never touch me or break me. Why? Because, I am unbreakable.

Sitting in this cell where I dwell, dreaming of freedom from this land of hell.

See, I was lost in confusion, ignorant and blind to the laws of justice.

Where I allowed the system to straight pimp me.

Use and abuse my mind and intelligence.

My momma didn't raise no fool, but somehow I became one.

The demons that haunted me started to take control over me.

Paralyzing my thoughts and intuition that was distilled within.

So I began to look for shelter, but shelter wasn't there to keep me warm.

I became a rebel without a cause, strapped with a 45, ready to take on all.

Ain't got time for no shucking and jiving.

Put the money in the bag before I start blasting.

I met two strangers, Pain and Anger, who became my friends

With every breath I took I was slowly losing the battle within.

And I will be damned if I was broke looking like a joke without no ends.

I see cats with big faces steady rollin' on them thangs that be spinnin.'

God forgive me I am a terrible sinner.

I was falling fast with the jaws of death clinging to my ass.

I tried to fight but the hounds who gave chase were too strong too fast.

It's strange how a man can lose himself fighting an enemy he cannot see.

Being blinded to the facts, he loses the empowerment of who he could be.

God give me strength and salvation take me into your loving arms give me peace,

Give me love. Give me new wing to fly high, fresh and reborn.

I am unbreakable Lord please guide me through this storm.

FIGHT THE POWER

Three years had passed by and things were starting to get out of control. Another Christmas and New Year's had come and gone. Holidays were the hardest time in prison. You see, all the Christmas commercials and it gets you sick to your stomach every time. The last thing you wanted to hear was some *Jingle bells.* The jail thought they were doing you a favor by providing, you with a turkey dinner and give you a few extra minutes to eat it.

I disliked eating the food in prison, because one, you got some creeps back there in the kitchen making your food. Two, some of them don't even take showers so why would I want them preparing my food. And three, soy products in foods taste horrible. When you're consuming general processed soy, it's like playing Russian roulette. Genetically, modified foods are linked to many health problems because they kill off good bacteria in your gut, known as probiotics benefits, and all the workings of your digestive system.

I was trying to survive. I saw the deadly game the Government was playing. They say reading is fundamental, I agree because for me it was a lifesaving. I started reading everything that I could get my hands on. Milk was another bad habit I had to get rid of. All my life I was told milk does a body good. But I started thinking if a kitten drinks cat milk and a puppy drinks dog milk. Why in the hell is a cow's milk good for humans? Something just didn't make sense. Again I did more research. For years, cow's milk has been claimed to be a go to source of calcium by the dairy industry. Some evidence suggests that consumption of milk and other dairy products leads to an increased risk of prostate cancer. Many cows are pumped full of antibiotics so imagine what comes out in the milk. Long story short, I was done with milk.

May 9, 2004 2 pm

I had been placed in SEG 30 days for punching a skinhead and maybe I kicked him a few times when he was down. People can talk to you until they're blue in the face, but what you will not do is disrespect me. I was passing out trays to our cellblock, because we were on lock down. A well-known racist skinhead on the deck named Rabbit wanted me to close his door for him. I explained to him I didn't close doors that was the Officer's job. He jumped up and said, "Nigger boy, you do what I tell you to do." That was the wrong thing to say and he paid for it severely. By the time several officers pulled me off of him, his blood was spilled. The jail was in an up rise, Aryan Nation and other white pride groups had made themselves known and there was a lot of tension.

I never understood how you could hate someone because the color of their skin. Black people, we were far from racist people, we love hard it was in our DNA. This was not my first run in with racist white pride groups. Unfortunately, it wouldn't be my last time. It was a damn shame a black man had to endure racism and bigotry in the free world. He also had to tolerate it on the inside even more. Even in prison, whites had better jobs than blacks. Blacks were the kitchen help or the broom and mop workers. While whites worked in warehouses, commissary, maintenance and the officer's kitchen. I still had a difficult time dealing with racism and to be in Southern Illinois, it was bad. A lot of the officers were rednecks and they didn't mind telling you what they thought about black people.

The day I got out of SEG, I got my property and everything was damaged. my fan, hot pot, headphones, radio and food. I was pissed and asked to speak to a white shirt. A white shirt is a Lieutenant that oversees its staff. When he saw all of the damaged property he kept it real. He told me they had a lot of wacky racist staff members. It didn't serve me well getting in a fight with a skinhead. He took an inventory of the damaged goods and said the jail would replace them. When you're locked down a man has nothing but his belongings and they're worth fighting for. However, this was unacceptable and uncalled for. His officers shouldn't be destroying inmates' property. This was the other part of the game these people play.

I can't say all C. O's were bad because they were not. I met a few who I was jammed tight with. I had a lot of rank in my organization and cops knew I kept the deck peaceful. So coming to work they felt safe. They could do their 8 hours and go home without any major hiccup. Some of these officers would work double shifts. They were at work more than home. So we weren't the only one's doing time. When you think about it, they were doing time also. The only difference was they got paid more than we did. But they still had to see the madness every day like we had to endure.

Racial tension had escalated between the whites and the blacks. There were huge fights in the chow halls and on the yard. I believe a lot of these incidents could've been avoided had, they removed certain radical whites who were nothing but troublemakers. If blacks were openly racist, they would've been on the first thing smoking, headed to a Maximum security prison. IDOC ran a tight ship. They believed in segregation; keep the blacks away from the whites. I was having small talk with a white inmate and he told me his uncle used to tell him don't never let a colored touch you. I replied, "Why?"

"Because you will never be able to get the dirt off," he said.

It was idiotic comments like that that made me wish I could meet his uncle so I could rub some of this black on him. Then he too would be dirty. I felt the need to teach this young man instead of getting angry.

"Listen, what if black people treated white people less than dogs. Raped your kids, your women and made you slaves. If that wasn't enough, murdered you at will and hung white men from trees. Whatever you created they took and claimed they made it. You couldn't eat in restaurants or look a black man in the eye. Black police officers pulled you over and claimed you were reaching for a gun and they shot and killed you. How about you apply for that good job to feed your family and you didn't get it because you were a white man?"

"Wow! I never looked at it like that," he said wide eye.

"Well every white person should look at it like that. But they don't. Most of them can't relate to what black people go through in this country on a daily basis. The media portrays black men as if we were animals, thugs and killers. They got us on the evening news every night showing you we are bad people nothing but criminals. But what they don't show you is what, Billy Bob did. He raped a 4-year-old little girl but you won't see his crime on the Evening News. Catholic Priest, have been molesting little white boys forever. Do you see them in prison? The reason why white people are fearful of blacks is because they know what they did to black people was horrendous. They want black people to forget and move on. To this day they refuse to admit any wrongdoing about slavery. Black people need closure. We don't need pity. In America every ethnic race has a little village, they can call home; Chinatown, Jew town, Little Italy, Puerto Ricans, Mexicans, Polish, Dutch, Hindus etc. Black people have nothing and every time we try to build something the government goes out of their way to shut it down. In our community, they give us poor schools, drugs and guns. In white communities you have good schools, river walks and nice parks with no broken bottles and kids aren't getting shot on the playground."

“Bro you got a point. I’m not going to lie, you guys got it tough.”

“Yeah it ain’t easy wearing this black skin because every day outside my window the Black Rain is always coming down.”

“Wow that’s deep bro.”

It was almost lock up time and I was heading for the shower. I put two guys on the shower for security. I wasn’t worried about nothing but at the end of the day safety always comes first. I was back in my cell when I heard a bunch of commotion. I quickly slid into my shoes and went into the day room to see what was going on. Inmates were arguing with officers and it looked like it was about to get ugly. I moved a couple of my guys out of harm’s way. The door had locked and one of the officers was still locked inside with us.

One of the Stones started fighting three officers out by the bubble. More officers came and they bum rushed him pretty good. At this time, about 40 or 50 inmates were yelling obscenities and banging on the glass. I knew the deck was going to go up in flames. The lone officer, I felt for him, he looked terrified as inmates turned on him than started attacking. It looked like a pack of wild Hyenas taking a bite out of its prey.

It didn’t take long for them to grab their man and pull him out of harm’s way. He was lucky to get out in one piece. I knew what was coming and it wasn’t going to be good. Guys were refusing to lock up; some of them were ready to go to war. One thing I knew is you can't fight a war you have no chance at winning. But it was so much unfairness going on guys was just tired, so they lashed out with what they knew violence.

Moments later officers came in the with their riot gear, Unit 1 was placed on a level 1 lock down. This was not good. A level 1 lock down meant you were in your cell 24/7 and there is no movement. By law they have to give you one shower every 7 days. The officers were pissed because one of their Officers was mauled. So when they passed out food trays in the morning you were missing items. One guy had a waffle on his tray and that was it. We were placed on lock down for three months. No commissary except for hygiene items. Guys who they thought were a threat was shipped to Menard or Pontiac.

I was tired and I was ready to leave Shawnee, but every 6 months I would put in for a transfer and be denied. I went to the Asst. Warden, Ms. Windsor to see what I could do to get out of their joint. I mean if I really wanted to get out here on a one-way ticket I had a couple of choices. One, I could go over to the officers I didn't like and punch him in the eye. Two, I could become a problem and force them to get rid of me. I had a lot on mind. I had another court motion I was working hard on. If I'm in SEG I can't go to the Law Library to work on my case.

One afternoon, I was coming from the library while my crazy unit, 1D, was coming back from the chow hall. A sergeant on the walk had collapsed from a heart attack. He was being wheeled out on a stretcher. I knew the sergeant and he happened to be a decent man. Some of the young and dumb inmates from my wing started clapping loudly, celebrating. I shook my head in disgust, because I knew what was coming. Sure enough the Captain came on the wing and locked it down. Thirty minutes later twenty-five inmates were pulled from their cell and put on a bus and shipped to Menard. The sad thing was they didn't even get the main ones who started the clapping.

We were placed on lockdown for another month. It's hard to hold your sanity when you are in a place of unrest. I didn't have any control over what was going on. I took my lumps like the rest and kept it moving.

IT'S A HARDKNOCK LIFE

I had six years left to go and each year was getting harder. I was missing my family like crazy. My baby girl Sharon had just written me a letter. She has been in my corner since day one and her letters always brought me joy. I laughed every time she asks me do I need anything. I always reply no because I'm the one who has always been the provider.

It's hard watching the ones you love living without you. This game of life was one big mystery and in order to solve the case you have to be ready for the challenge each and every day. Malcolm X once said, "A man is entitled to make a fool of himself if he's ready to pay the cost."

I was still sort of feeling my way out. I was starting to go through cellies like water. Today I got a new celly and he just got out of SEG. I was sitting on the bottom bunk listening to Carl Thomas's *Summer Rain* when he came in. This guy was huge about 6'7 270. The first thing he asked me is the bottom bunk was for sale? Immediately, I sprang to my feet and gave him a few choice words to let him know there was nothing in here for sale. A man will test you to see where you stand. One thing about being in prison, you never know the next man's intention, you question everything, and you check every door. If a man thinks he can buy you; deep down he won't be able to respect you.

I watched as my new celly climbed his 6'8 frame on the top bunk, unknowingly to him, in my mind I had already sized him up. See one thing you learn about living in a tight space with the enemy is you have to always be one step ahead of them. In case we ever had to do battle I had to be mentally and physically prepared at all cost. If not, I could be seriously injured or even killed.

I had hundreds of cellmates and I rarely ever trusted one. Men in prison get raped and killed in their cells all the time. This guy was top heavy and had skinny legs. So if I had to do battle I would hit him low like chopping down a tree. Mentally, he wasn't that sharp. He just met me and in three hours I knew everything about him. Where he's from, where he lived, his charges, girlfriend, baby mama, out date, etc. This guy was telling me everything I did not ask for. I know the cops probably loved this guy.

Sometimes man is his own worst enemy because if he's constantly opening his mouth just like a fish he's going to get caught. Being incarcerated opened my eyes not only to learning about myself, but also my black brothers. Sadly, I had met well over a thousand men behind bars. By far black men were the most dominant in the school of the hard knocks. We were very creative, hard workers, resourceful and we showed genuine love just to name a few. But where we fail at were our mindsets. Our minds could be easily highjack you don't need a gun to highjack a person's mind. All it takes is a slick tongue that can dance with its shoes off. A slick tongue can be enticing; it looks and sounds good. If the mind proceeds, then you will do what the mind tell you to do.

Sometimes I felt like a fly on the wall, I wasn't physically here, but my eyes and ears were. I closely paid attention to everything around me. I was that 5-year-old kid again on the South Side of Chicago. At times, I could be proud of my brothers and other times I wanted to choke the living life out of them. When a man knows what buttons to push he keeps pushing them. We often tend to play on other people's emotions and some of us are always searching for the next come-up. Every opportunity doesn't need to be taken advantage of. Sometimes we have to look the other way.

Black men are God's chosen people. We are not niggers or niggas. We are gods that's why we have been blessed abundantly with so many gifts. The powers at be, knows this information and they hate it. So they will do anything to destroy that image. Even Adolf Hitler knew the truth. He stated, "The Americans have the jewels of God. They have stolen God's precious jewels. The Negroes. They are the true Hebrews." You won't learn this in a history book in school. The truth is out there if you're willing to search for it.

Can you imagine sports, music, movies, or life in general without the black man? I see beauty in all people. But when it comes to black people, I see why we are God's chosen people. I only wished my people did. However, until we learn who we are, where we come from, and what we are capable of; it will continue to be a struggle to live, a struggle to survive.

One thing I know about being a black man is once we set our minds to do something we do it. Right or wrong we are on a mission. But sometimes our mission is not clear, and we can't keep jumping out a plane without a parachute. I know a lot of black men are emotional because we were, raised by a woman and I'm one of them. Most of our fathers weren't around to show us how to beat on our chest. A boy needs his father to walk him into manhood. When times get tough; his boots will be tied up. The best gift a man can give to his seed is water.

In prison, I saw so many young brothers aimlessly running around like chickens with their heads cut off. They were all over the place and some of them can't even read or write. They spend most of their time rappin' trying to be the next Lil Wayne. They don't keep their hygiene up nor do they respect their elders. I had this young 19-year-old cellmate who was from the wild-wild hundreds, far South Side of Chicago. He only had eight days left before his release date. He had just got out of SEG. The kid was rail thin and his mouth was louder than a motor. I explained to him everyone that lives in my cell has to wash, their hands. It was mandatory that they clean up after themselves. We are grown men so we must act like men.

My fear in prison was dying there from a horrible disease that came from germs. Staph infection and Mercer were common. A sweet old lady, who work in health care caught the bug and died three weeks later. Most staph bacteria are transmitted via, person to person contact. I wasn't going to go out like that so I made sure everything around me was clean, including cellmates.

Everything this kid had was full of filth; clothes, shoes, and bed sheets. I paid to wash everything he had because there was no way I was going to be able to stomach his filth. I tried talking to the young brother but it was a lost cause. The kid was wild and he thought his way was the right way.

One night I was sitting up watching Monday night football and out of nowhere the kid bellowed out, "if we were slaves I would be in the house and you would be in the field."

It took everything in me not to bust out in laughter. I guess he feels because he has light skin that he was better than me. I sat up and gave him a side-eye look. It's obvious he didn't have the slightest idea who I was. Because if he had, he wouldn't have fixed his lips to say something stupid like this.

"Do you want to have an intelligent conversation because I don't do foolish conversations?" I told him.

He stood by the door gazing out at the day room. "That's real talk. Light skin is where it's at I get plenty of hoes in the world. They don't even mess with dark skinned niggas."

See this was the problem with so many ignorant young brothers, they were like fools, testing the water with both feet. I gave him a Willie Lynch quote, "I have outlined a number of differences among the slaves and these differences I take and make them bigger. I use fear, distrust and envy for control purpose. What you believe in your head is the seed Willie Lynch planted in our people. If you divide the strongest race of people, they will never form unity and reap the benefits of their dominance. The reason why the white man would prefer you in the house isn't because of you have light skin, it's because you would be more content with pleasing the masta and kissing his ass. Dark skinned men like me, they didn't trust because they knew if push came to shove we would kill their asses. Understand black people were enslaved for over 200 years, during which, we were not considered to be human. Your light skin tone came from the black women in your family being raped as young as 12 years old. If you're happy to be light skin remember your mom's mom, mom paid the price for your skin color. It's a shame the residue of the "house" versus the "field negro" divide is still alive amongst us. If you look at some of the darker brothers today that anger over the old distinction is still there. Because we know our dark skin gets unfair treatment. White people to this day get scared or intimidated when they see a large dark skin brother walking toward them. They think we got super powers or we will take something from them. Listen young buck, get your head inside a book and understand what you are up against."

"Man I don't care about all that garbage that was before my time. I'm living for today," he said in an even tone.

"Damn living for today if you can't prepare for tomorrow."

"Man, you old head's be trying to sound like y'all know everything. If y'all know everything why y'all in jail?" He yelled.

"Look shorty lower your voice! We men up in here."

"Shorty? I got your shorty pimpin," he said coldly, quickly sliding his feet into his gym shoes. In prison when a man slides his feet into his shoes: 1. He is either going somewhere or 2. He is ready to do battle.

I looked at the kid as he was putting on his shoes to fight. He was running his mouth talking about how he be treating old cat's down here. By the time he got his second foot in his shoes, I was on him like a bad nightmare. I placed both of my hands around his swan neck and lifted his feet up off the floor. I applied ample amount of pressure to let him know I could snap him in two.

"Who do you think you are little punk? I will kill you up in here, is this what, you want? Huh punk?" I yelled with venom dripping from my mouth.

"Big homie. Big homie, I'm cool. I'm cool big homie."

I was inches away from nearly beating the hell out of this young kid. I shook him like a rag doll flinging his rail thin body from side to side. I didn't take threats lightly. If a man aggressively challenges you, you have to respond accordingly. It didn't dawn on me until I saw the look of terror in his bloodshot eyes. I let him loose because I could've easily snapped his windpipe.

"Big homie, I apologize bro," he sobbed as his frame slid down the wall.

I took a step back and caught my breath. The man I once was always seems to pop up unexpectedly. Every day I was learning the war within was a fight within itself. I hated to lose my cool, but when you're in hell the devil loves to play. Now it dawned on me why these people put this kid in my cell with 8 days left to go home. He had a big mouth and they wanted someone to give him a nice beating before he went home. They knew my track record and they figured a guy who's known to fight, will definitely give him what he was looking for. That was the nature of the beast they had hidden ways to make you comply. Some guys loved to give a guy a nice shiner before they went home especially if they didn't like the guy. One of the golden rules that was a lost art was never tell anyone your outdate.

"Cooley you good?" A brother asked peeping into the cell.

"Yeah everything is good." I responded.

I felt bad for the kid. I gave him a long heartfelt conversation and this time he was paying attention. I told him if you keep looking for the big bad wolf you will find him. There are dos to life and there are don't s. This kid was going to have to find out the hard way. This was a learning moment for him. My old self would've reacted in a violent way, but I was pleased I was able to reframe myself and remain cool like the other side of a pillow. In the hard knock life there are no rules; low blows count too.

BROTHER'S

I've *seen* brothers who didn't take showers or brush their teeth or comb their hair.

I've seen brothers who sell their soul for a dollar that made me wanna holla.

I've seen brothers who couldn't read or write, but loved to fight.

I've seen brothers cuss their momma with the same mouth

turn-around and kiss another brother in the mouth.

I've seen brothers kill brothers with words that touches nerves

now the same brothers are lying sleep and can't be reached.

I've seen brothers who helped brothers who couldn't help themselves.

I've seen brothers who loved brothers when no one else was there.

Brothers my brothers; I wish we could go back to being brothers.

I CAN'T BELIEVE

Lately I had so much on my mind. I couldn't think straight long enough to sort out my issues. Sometimes in life a man has to go through it and see for himself it wasn't meant for him. I know in my heart of hearts God didn't intend for me to be a prisoner stuck behind bars. I knew somewhere there was a life out there for me and I promised God if He delivered me from my old way of thinking I would not disappoint Him.

I began to manifest my new life and it didn't involve prison. My mind was far from this crazy place and I began putting my new life together. The pen became my new friend. It all started when I was placed in SEG for allegedly disobeying an officer's direct order. For years, this officer always had a problem with me. I guess because so many, of his fellow officers respected me including female officers. Majority of the officers always called me by my nickname "Cooley." So I was highly accepted in their world; a place here an inmate had no business. However, when the black assistant warden got wind of my circumstances, he immediately had me released from SEG. I lost my job working from operations, but I did gain a friend in the pen.

I was listening to Jay Z's "The Blue Print" and thought it would be a good idea to put my own blue print together. I wrote down everything from how I would dress, to someday owning my own business. I was going to be an author by all means. My favorite scripture of the Bible is Philippians 4:13 *I can do all things through Christ which strengthen me.* I wholeheartedly believed in Christ and I knew through him all things were possible.

The first day I was in SEG, a voice I did not know whispered to me over the shoulder. "It's time for you to write." Immediately I bolted up from my bunk looking around the cell. A chill of excitement had claimed me as the tiny hairs on my forearms began to dance. Normally, when I would write something I discarded it, but not this time. The ink from my pen flowed freely tapping into a place where there was nothing but bliss. It felt good to travel in the world of my imagination. Exploring images and concepts of external objects not present to the senses was refreshing.

That day I created my first short story called "The Back Breaker," the life of an exotic male dancer. I can't believe the burst of energy that was running through my veins. Finally, I had found something deep inside of me that was special and dear. I read and reread the story again and again. I was amazed on how well the story flowed. It flowed like a red rose heading gently down a stream. Everything was written beautifully and for the first time in my life I let someone else read my work other than myself. That person deep inside is the one who knew, but we, as people tend to keep that burning desire hidden. We all have dreams and passion but if we don't give them a voice no one will hear them speak.

So many entities were coming at me in unusual ways. If my mind wasn't strong enough to keep out the unwanted residents, I knew there was no possible way that my mind would be sane. One of my mottos was, don't let people rent space in your head for free. Everything in your mind must make sense. You don't do anything for nothing. There's always an answer for a question. People are always searching for the truth, but sometimes the truth, don't want to be found.

A person in prison suffers from extreme hardship. When you are stripped of everything, including your name and dignity then placed in chains and shackles, the word state property comes to life. Humans referred to as state property can be traced back to the roots of slavery. Plantations housed slaves. Prisons house black folks. Who were the slaves? *The black folks*. Although some people may strongly disagree and say prisons are not the new plantations. I beg to differ because I am here live, in the flesh on the front line buddy. They don't actually force you into slavery, but they place so many barriers in your path that will lead you into slavery. It's a difficult road we travel and the Black Rain keeps coming and never ceases to let up.

When you think about it was a brilliant plan. White people are not smarter than us, they just tend to out think us. They play dirty while we march and protest asking for fairness. We live in a country that wasn't founded on fairness. We must wake up and understand who and what we are dealing with. History has a way of repeating itself. When the other side gets threatened they look for blood because they understand war is necessary. In the past, I couldn't think straight I had so much hate and bitterness in my heart it almost destroyed me. What you don't understand you're not always willing to except. When it comes to racism in this country, people keep pretending the elephant in the room is not there.

I guess today I was feeling some type of way. Even though I was down I still wore a smile on my face. My federal habeas corpus was denied in the federal courtroom. Lisa Madigan's office really stuck it to me. A Federal habeas corpus is a procedure under which a federal court may review the legality of an individual's incarceration. I've been through the State of Illinois, The Appellate Court, the Supreme Court and now Federal. I couldn't believe they denied me once again.

Every denied motion felt like a punch in the gut that hurt for a couple of days. The system is not set up for the poor and unrepresented to be successful. You may have a legit claim where there was a violation of your due process but the fact that you are poor and you are behind bars; the system tends to purposely deny your claim hoping that you will give up the fight. I have had so many motions denied I have lost count. Not only has this happened to me but I have seen it happen to other inmates also. It takes your will and makes you no longer want to fight. However, I had to stay strong no matter what and keep it moving.

Prison had a way of dulling your spirit and depleting your energy. Guys were walking around like the living dead daily. Some of them would try anything to escape from their reality by taking drugs when they didn't need them. Sleeping pills and Xanax were heavy favorites. Guys would do anything to get those meds even play crazy. They figured if they were high or sleep they wouldn't have to deal with their bid. Every time meds came around guys were lined up like a dope stop waiting for their fix to put them in la-la land. I looked at prison with sad eyes, because I saw it for what it was. It was a dark, underground world with lost souls trapped looking for a way out. Some were looking to be saved; others wanted to continue to roam.

They say where your mail is delivered is your place of residence. I will never claim prison as my home. Some guys did that, that's why they kept returning. The way I see it everybody makes mistakes in life, as long as you don't make a mistake you can't come back from, you will have a chance to turn your life around. With a strong mindset you can bounce back from anything. No matter what these people or these evil forces try to do to you in here, they will never be able to touch your mind or dampen your spirit. If you don't, let them. *Stay strong!*

A WOMAN'S TOUCH

My long days were filled with lonely nights and not having a woman to romance was starting to take its toll on me. A man that's manly needs that oneness that he can only get from a woman. I'd been locked up for almost 9 years and hadn't felt the tender sweet caress of a woman's touch. That alone left an ache a man couldn't suppress. Behind bars when it comes to women a man has his photographic memory. The ones he misses the most are the ones he visits when he's alone.

Fall was here and I couldn't wait to scratch another year off the calendar. One morning, I went to the yard and got some shots up on the basketball court. Then I ran 2 miles. My team was playing in the championship game tomorrow afternoon against a tough opponent. The last time we played them, I scored 44 points and we still lost. When it came to basketball, I still had the burning desire as kid trying to be Michael Jordan. I used basketball along with my writing to escape the everyday madness. Over the years I had enhanced my skill level on the basketball court where I was arguably the best shooter in the joint. Every 3-point contest I had been in. I won.

Being good in basketball did have its perks. In Southern Illinois the C.Os loved their St. Louis Cardinals and their Southern Illinois Salukis. So they enjoyed watching me play. Sometimes they would give me 2 or 3 gym periods just to see me play against the other competition. Every time I stepped on the court I made sure I represented Aurora (A-town). Chicago inmates thought they were better than everyone else. So I had to prove them wrong. It was a battle and I welcome the competition.

I can't believe we had Keon Clark down here. Two years ago I was watching him play in the NBA on TV. How could you be in the NBA one moment and the next moment you are in prison? It's called life. One or two bad decisions can change your life it didn't matter who you were. Prison was real. For me playing basketball was my outlet. It was the only time I didn't feel like I was incarcerated. Of course, when your good at anything you do, you're gonna have your fair share of haters. Jealousy and envy is real.

While I was coming off the yard one of my biggest fans was walking toward me. Her name was Miss C. She was a female Correction Officer. I'm not going to lie she had my nose wide open. The smell of her sweet fragrance made me want to dip my nose into the curl of her neck. She was a white woman built like a sister, thick thighs and a round bottom that was appeasing to the eye. She was cute and every time we saw each other the predatory stares were getting more intense.

"Hey Cooley," she said in passing, her pink cheeks blushing.

"What up, Miss C," I waved giving her the eye.

It was obvious something was there between us. I remember her first day on the job 6 years ago. She was young and fresh. Every thirsty man in this camp wanted her. One thing about male C.Os, they were trying to smash the women too. If they saw a woman, giving an inmate the eye, they were going to make that inmates life even more difficult. In prison, relationships between an inmate and staff member happens more often than you would think. I am a witness. I witnessed it with my own eyes. However, if caught, you would pay a substantial price and get more time added to your sentence.

After we won the championship game, Miss C started working in my building, and every time I looked around her eyes were all on me. Of course other inmates knew she had a strong liking for me. So I had to be careful on how I moved. She even got bold and would come in my cell and sit on my bed and watch T.V. She was definitely making it hard for me. The more she came around the more I wanted her.

Behind bars, when dealing with a woman that you are not supposed be dealing with you have to wait for her to initiate the contact. If you shoot your shot and it gets rejected she could have you locked up and shipped to another joint for reckless eyeballing or inappropriate sexual misconduct. There is a fine line you have to walk inside these walls to stay out of harm's way. Whatever you do you must keep to yourself you can't even talk to the walls because the walls have ears. In here men gossip like women and they will tell on you just for the hell of it. Cat's now didn't need a reason to tell, they told freely. More than 70% of prisons are infested with guys who like to play let's make a deal.

When I first came into prison there was structure, the gangs ran the joint. Now there is no structure, it's every man for himself the floodgate is now open.

One thing about Miss C she always valued and respected my opinion. She would always run her problems by me and I would give her useful advice she could fall back on. One day I was on the basketball court and a guy kept fouling me on purpose because he couldn't stop me. In my anger, I threw the ball at him and got in his face. Miss C yelled and broke it up. She sent the other guy back to his housing unit and I was allowed to continue to play ball. Afterward, she kept me in the gym by myself and she gave me some friendly advice. We were all along not a soul in sight.

"I can't have you out here going to SEG," she said with a serious face.

"SEG is just another part of the jail," I chuckled.

She walked over to me and looked up into my brown eyes. "If you in that other part of the jail you can't get this," she smiled raising her lips to smother mine.

I wrapped my arms around her like a blanket and pulled her softness into my hard body. Our tongues danced wildly enjoying each other's warm cavity. The fire on the stove was hot and the pot was boiling. I could feel the quakes in her limbs as her body became warm and inviting. I couldn't turn back now because I fell in. I was hot and wet and I was dripping.

I can't deny she had me spellbound caught up in lust and loneliness. This was a showdown that was long overdue. Her touch sent a jolt of electricity that made more than the tiny hairs on the back of my neck stand up. I pushed her back against the wall and greedily devoured her. Her breathing intensified and I enjoyed every moment. It's been a long time since a woman made me feel this alive.

That night mark the beginning of stormy romance. There's nothing like a woman's touch even in the land of darkness. Her touch can mean so much. However, I knew I was setting myself up for a downfall. But at the time everything felt so right. When everything is so right you go with it and hope it's right. I was allowing my lower region to lead and when he leads, he leads. When he leads all hell may break loose.

Days later she made every excuse to be around me. When my celly went to chow or after she does count. Things were getting a little dicey. She was starting to get too attached and that could end in a disaster. I pulled her to the side and read her, her rights. I told her she had to slow down or she was going to crash and kill us both.

I'M GOING DOWN

Another year was gone and I was closer to the gate. I had just started writing my first book and it was coming along well. It was called "Head or Tails" a street novel by Cooley. I had written hundreds of poems and letters not only for myself but for others as well. Writing for me was not only therapeutic it was also profitable. I was writing poems and selling them to a Christian Publishing Company in Carbondale. Here in the joint, I was killing them softly, charging them by the page. I was the man to go to when you couldn't think or write for yourself. It was a nice hustle that kept me busy.

January 13,

Today I got a letter from my Pops who lives on the South Side of Chicago. He wanted to wish me a Happy New Year. My Pops was cool, even though he wasn't always there for me when I was a kid. I don't hold a grudge against him. I still had a descent upbringing. I knew wrong from right and every bad decision I made I had no one to blame but myself. When a man recognizes his mistakes he doesn't make excuses, he corrects them. I had a lot of correcting to do.

From day one of my incarceration my Pops has been there every step of the way. He showed up in crunch time and helped me get up off the floor. For that, I will forever be grateful. So I don't care who they say my father was, the only thing that matters is who he is to me.

****

March 10, 2008

Its late couldn't sleep the pen needed to speak!

QUEEN

Cloudy days filled with sleepless nights,

I toss and turn trying to contemplate my thoughts.

When I first met her, I felt that feeling of desire.

You know the kind that set your soul on fire.

Words are indescribable, the passion I felt for this woman.

I was her Ashford and she was my Simpson

Together we made beautiful music. Our love was solid.

Solid as a rock!

Her skin was dark and beautiful, eyes danced, with romance, lips were full and succulent.

To taste her I would die for.

To know her I would love her.

Her smile was the essence that captured my heart.

It was like the sun rising over the horizon giving me its warmth of its glow.

Feeling my soul with a sensation of joy.

This woman made me feel alive

Feeding my heart with a new vibe.

When she touched my hand, my flesh became weak.

She seduced me in a way my mind could not explain.

I was lost in confusion but I was dying to taste nectar of her sweet passion.

To bury my bone, deep to quench the thirst that harassed me.

I wanted to take her in my arms and love her.

Be her knight in shining armor and protect her.

I'm glad the men who didn't cherish her

Left her for a man like me to marry her.

They didn't know how to treat a woman that was worth

more than buried treasure.

God sent me an angel and a smile back from heaven.

Her regal crown fits her head perfectly

I see her clearly like a photo I can touch

She can't see me through the storm, because it rains so much.

My eyes are wide-open blessed to be able to see.

It won't be long my Queen; your King will soon be free.

I love writing poetry, because if you couldn't be the poem, be the poet. Langston Hughes was by far my favorite poet. The Weary Blues and the Negro Speaks of Rivers were some of my favorite pieces. Hughes was one of the earliest innovators of the then-new literary art form called jazz poetry. Words are like a treasure and the more you gather them up the bigger your treasure will grow. Deep thoughts put you on another level with the universe. God gave humans a vision. There's nothing more powerful than a vision. We need to release our positive energy in the world and watch it come back in full. My thoughts were on the world and the last part of my blueprint was my Queen. I envisioned a woman that was going to be

God fearing, loyal, and beautiful inside and out. I was no longer going to associate myself with women *who didn't believe in me or support my vision. I knew I had this huge ball of energy left in me that needed to be released.* My queen was out there somewhere and one day I will find her.

Miss C. was removed from our Unit and she sent a kite through another officer to let me know what was going on. I read the letter and couldn't believe she had another officer deliver it to me. I was heated because this chick knew the heat was on. I.A. had already called me over asking questions. They just had hearsay, but they did let me know if they get anything solid I was gone.

For months, I was walking around on thin ice hoping it wouldn't break. They finally moved me out of my Unit after 5 years. They were trying to shake me up and it was coming from the higher up. One of the Lieutenants had a thing for Miss C. and to hear my name pop up he was going to do whatever to make me uncomfortable.

Two weeks later I was on the move again this time to Unit 4. Unit 4 was the house that housed all the troublemakers. Every week this house was subject to be on lock down. These were the type of games these people played. *I got the power. I will crush you.* I think every law enforcement agent has played that power card. But it didn't take long for them to piss me off again. The very next week I was headed to Unit 2. Unit 2 was the schoolhouse wing and kitchen workers. Even though I hated I had to tuck my tail, but I knew one man could not defeat an army. A man has to choose his battles wisely and every battle wasn't worth fighting. It doesn't make you less than a man not to respond or react to every situation that comes your way. I learned a cool head wins in the end.

June 27, 2008

Nothing got better and nothing changed. I stayed out of the line of fire as long as I could. Today is my third day in SEG. I was charged with having a makeshift weapon in my property. Of course the charges were bogus. I tried pleading my case to one of the lieutenants who I knew very well and I considered him a fair man. He told me it was out of his hands and there was nothing he could do. I pissed off the wrong people and they wanted my head on a platter. Everyone knew about the fling I had going on with Miss C, and she didn't do me any justice by coming around every night hanging on my door over here in SEG. One thing I could say about her is she genuinely cared for me and that I appreciated. However, this was not my world and one day I will rise from these ashes to become what I'm supposed to be. Prison is for losers; men who accepted defeat. Some of these guys minds were already made up they could not win. The belly of the beast will swallow you up, but only the strong will survive and get spit out.

I sat in SEG for months and today I finally found out they were shipping me to, Pinckneyville Correctional Center. I had mixed feelings about going to Pinckneyville, but there was nothing I could do. The Board didn't know what to make of the fictitious charges. They were even scratching their head trying to figure out what to do. Hopefully the way I spoke and articulated my words, they would see the man and not the prisoner. Shawnee requested I get a year across the board. That meant I would lose a year that I already served. I was hotter than hot coals. These people had nothing on me but some trumped up charges. I don't know how that make shift weapon got in my box, but I didn't put there, never seen it before. Somehow I had to think my way out of this jam because I could not afford to take an L on these charges.

"Aye Cooley," a C.O. tapped on my cell door.

"Wassssup?" I replied.

"Hey I got to pull you out for a second," he said jiggling the bracelets in front of his face.

I shook my head. *What the hell these people want from me now?*

He placed the cuffs on my wrist and led me down the hallway and around the corner. Miss C was all smiles waiting for me. She gave me a long hug and told me I will be on the move soon. She smelled real nice as always. I couldn't lie I was going to miss this woman and maybe in another life who knows what would've happen. Sometimes I could be my own worst nightmare and that always troubled me. I kissed her on the cheek and nuzzled her pink nose. "Be good," I grinned. Then turned and walked away.

"You too handsome, and no more fighting on the basketball court," she chuckled.

For what's it worth, I never saw her again and that was fine by me. I had too much on my plate I wasn't trying to eat. I wish nothing but the best for her. But it was time for me to get back to being focused. A man who couldn't focus won't accomplish too much of anything. I closed that chapter in my book and I was ready move on to the next one.

Three days later, I was dressed, chained and shackled in a tan colored jumpsuit with the letters SEG engraved on my back. I had just boarded a bus to Pinckneyville Correctional Center. I was getting dropped off first so they placed me in the front seat by the window. I couldn't complain. I had the best seat on the bus besides the driver. My gaze immediately fell on the outside world as soon as the bus pulled off. It was 5 a.m. and a lot folks weren't out yet. This was the first time I saw the outside world in more than 7 years. *I see McDonald's hadn't changed they still serving a billion strong.* Wow looking at the outside world was like seeing and smelling good food you could not eat, so your stomach growls and you are left hungry. I made up mind when I get free I'm going to eat a lit bit of everything. God gives us so much but unfortunately some us won't live to see it because our eyes are still closed.

I was at a total loss for words, for me that's surprising because I'm a man with many words, it's been a long 7 years since I last smelled fresh air. The air inside the beast was stale and automatically I noticed the difference. Once you're locked up everything around you gets enhanced including your 5 senses. A man's nose was like a K-9 if a woman came near he could easily tell if her feminine hygiene was up to par. Oh yeah it gets deep. The mind of a man gets sharper if he chooses to sharpen it. I sat back and stared out the window ignoring the country music that was playing loudly out the speakers. Life is truly beautiful and here I was wasting it like a damn fool.

Pinckneyville was about an hour away. Like so many other prisons I've been to they all looked the same. Each housing unit was built into an X. They had 4 wings and a control tower was built in the center, which was, referred to as "the bubble." The bubble was the spot where officers sat back and watched everything you did. We like to refer to correctional officers as guards. Even though they may get resentful or annoyed for being called a guard, but when you think about it, it's the truth. Their job was to watch over and protect, and to control. We were like gold, and big business meant big money.

I am a numbers guy. When I sit back and watch all the billions of dollars being made off the backs of blacks and the poor. How in the world can someone, fix their lips to say slavery doesn't still exist? IDOC gets over 38,000 for each inmate a year. They have 25 adult correctional facilities that are only supposed to hold 32,000 inmates. There are almost 50,000 inmates. The numbers and overcrowding are sharply rising.

When I'm done serving my sentence the Department of Illinois Corrections are going to make a whopping 500,000 dollars just off of little ole me. Wow! The people who are getting beat are the American Taxpayers. *Suckers.* Prisons are nothing more than a Ponzi scheme set-up to bankroll the people and to keep blacks and the poor disenfranchise from attaining a good quality of life. The last thing they want to see is Ray-Ray telling their son Little Bobby you're fired. They see us as workers not Bosses. The more people they keep putting behind bars, the more money taxpayers will be paying. According to the National Association for the Advancement of Colored People (NAACP), African Americans constitute nearly 1 million of the total 2.3 million incarcerated populations, and have nearly six times the incarceration rate of whites. These numbers are mind-blowing.

If Blacks only make up 12-13 % of America's population there's no way in hell we should be the leading vote getters when it comes to mass incarceration. You can thank the first black President for that Mr. Bill Clinton. I never understood why we keep asking the masta for a piece of meat when he don't even want to give black folks crumbs to eat. We have to stop asking and start doing for self. We need all our young black men to fight the power with their minds not with stupidity. We wage war on each other because; we have been, bamboozled by the enemy. Put down the guns, pick up a book and read. Change the mindset of willing to die for your brother and learn to live for your brother. Even through the eyes of my youth I never believed in killing someone because of their gang affiliation. Gang banging was corny and stupid. If you were going to pledge your life to something let it be to your family. When you're doing a hundred years behind these brick walls or taking an early dirty nap. You will feel like a fool wishing you chosen a better route. Don't be that fool like I was live my brother live. The dope game was even more sinister. We are trick to believe selling poison to our people will make us wealthy. But in reality we're doing nothing but killing two birds with one stone. The dope pusher will eventually find his or her way into a prison cell or an early grave. The drug abuser will walk through hell feeding a demon that eats away at their soul.

I was taught to love all people, and if they didn't love you back, then that was their problem. We all were raised different but we should all share one common goal and that's to love each other. God gave us gifts to give to each other. The more we understand His purpose; we will begin to understand our own. That goes out to my brown brothers as well as my white brothers. We are one because we come from each other.

CHANGED MAN

I had just seen the Board yesterday and they told me they were not going to give me a year across the board. They gave me time served and will be letting me out of SEG on Thanksgiving Day. So that meant I had to sit in SEG for another 43 days. I was relieved about the parole board decision but to leave me in SEG for another 6 weeks, I was looking at them rather side-eyed. They based their decision on something that wasn't a weapon but if it would have been put together it could have been used as a weapon.

I've been in Pinckneyville for 3 weeks and this place was terrible. Officers talked to you in a very disrespectful manner, as if, though they had an "S" on their chest. I had to remind myself to breathe and relax. These people were not in my future. This was only temporary. However, my attention was tuned into the Presidential election. I was very excited that a black man had a chance to become President.

To be honest, I never thought this day would come in my lifetime or in any lifetime. This country was too full of hate and racism to give the black man the keys to the earth, but if it did happen, it will be an amazing time in American history. I would love to see a powerful moment that will show some of the young black men in this country anything was possible, even becoming President of the United States. If there were ever a great candidate to elect as the first black President, Barak Obama was the one. I liked him a lot. He spoke with great passion and deep concern for this country. If he wins, I just hope they don't assassinate him.

Being locked in Segregation was definitely no fun. Thank God I had a pen and sharp mind to keep me company. I had a Latino celly that came from Centralia Prison. He was a cook. He got caught with a sharp piece of metal he used to cut cards he made for holidays or birthdays. In prison, you have to have a hustle in order to eat. So I understand the grind because if you didn't have any money sent in from the world you were assed out. You had no choice but to hustle by all means. The stories this guy shared with me were made for TV. He was here from Mexico illegally and every time he got caught they deported him back to Mexico.

"So how did you get back over here?" I asked him.

"I paid a Coyote. I gave him three thousand."

"A Coyote?"

"A Coyote was a guy that got you over the border. He will stash you in a truck or stuff you in the back of a trunk. It's big business," he said.

"I see."

"I hate to go back over there and start all over again," he said sadly.

Listening to someone else's problems is what prisoners did. Sometimes we were all we had in time of need. Just when you think you had problems, someone else's problems were more complicated than yours. He had a family to support and they were counting on him when he returned. Now his future was bleak and so were the ones who depended on him.

Later that night I was awaken from loud voices. This was nothing new in the land of hell. As I peeked out my cell door window, I noticed a tall white shirt (LT) yelling at a young black inmate who was handcuffed. The young man said he felt suicidal. The LT didn't believe him, he felt the inmate was lying and wanted to get out of the cell from his cellmate. Inmates do pull the suicide card to get out a bad situation. However, what happen next made me want tear off the hinges of the steel door.

"So you wanna kill yourself you piece of shit?" The white shirt yelled."

"Yes sir," the inmate replied.

"Okay let's go. I'm going to help you. Let's go."

The white shirt angler face, redden as he slammed the handcuffed man face against the wall. Next he used the kid face as a rag as he wiped his face along the wall. The man screamed in terror as his head was being dragged along the wall and doors. Then as he got towards the stairs the white shirt pushed the handcuffed man down the stairs. The man feet couldn't catch up with his momentum, he fell head first, crashing to the floor on his face.

"You still want to kill yourself," the white shirt roared.

The young man cried out in agony as he was hoisted up off the floor by three officers and carried away. Other inmates kicked and screamed obscenities from behind their cell doors. It was an uproar we, were pissed. "Anybody else wanna kill themselves while, I'm here," he said with a devilish grin.

I was furious and at times like this I wouldn't mind having a piece of Mr. White Shirt. I stood in my stance by the door staring at drops of blood that were spilled on the floor. I get so sick and tired of being sick and tired. *How long must I keep watching the same damn movie? The black rain drips and drips.* Here I was trying my best to be a changed man. But the devil loves to dance.

There were so many evil souls roaming the earth, change was not going to come easy. I finally closed my eyes and put some pressure on my bunk. But my mind could not stop thinking about the heartless act I just witnessed. In my opinion, no man deserves to be treated less than a man. God created man equally but man sees things differently. A man in a powerful position has to be wise not foolish. Sadly, that's the way of the world too many men who were foolish had all the power.

JOY AND PAIN

"**H**e did it! He did it!" A gallery worker pushing a broom said in a low tone.

"He won?"

"Yep, man it was beautiful."

A huge smile lit up my face and tears that felt wet and warm begin to roll down my cheeks. *Wow, we had a Black President in the White House are you kidding me? That's awesome.* I couldn't believe my ears. Obama did it. He is the first Black President of the United States. Words were indescribable the joy I felt at this moment in my life. The warm tears I shed were not only for me, but it was for the Martin Luther Kings and Medgar Evers of the world who lost their lives fighting against injustice and bigotry. It was for my ancestors, who were hung from trees, beaten, raped, and mistreated. This day, November 5, 2008, is a day I will never forget as long as I live.

I remember when I first heard the guy who was from my old childhood neighborhood, Hyde Park speak for the very first time. I found Barak Obama funny, intelligent and very knowledgeable. I couldn't wait to hear more. Then when I read Obama's book, "The Audacity of Hope," I was impressed and blown away. I saw he was a very careful student of his unique journey and the stars were aligning in his favor. He was a smart man and when he opened his mouth he spoke eloquently and you loved everything he said. Obama was refreshing and honest. He will be good for the free world if given a chance to deliver.

News of a black man was going to be running the world had spread around the cellblock like a wildfire. Everybody was yelling out, their chuckholes. It felt good to see these men find some temporary relief from the madness. This was a joyful time for the black man. An ultimate victory, the dream of impossible is no longer a dream. A black man could be all things, even become the President of the United States. This was huge the biggest event of our lifetime.

I guess the powers that be did not approve of our little celebration. They turn up the blowers in each cell and the cold freezing air felt like you were standing in a blizzard. Inmates were screaming and beating on the doors with their fist. I was pissed along with them because the arctic air was too much to handle. Funny thing is, during the summer they hardly ever turn on the blowers. Over the intercom a C.O. yelled, "George W Bush is the President. Obama ain't shit." And there you have it. The little joy we get the enemy takes it away. Shouts of joyful praises were replaced with angry cuss words. I put on extra layers of clothes and threw a blanket around me trying to keep warm.

On Thanksgiving Day, I was finally let out of SEG. I had lost 15 pounds in 6 months. One thing about going to SEG you will lose weight. Getting adjusted to Pinckneyville was going to be tougher than I anticipated. Anything that happened the joint automatically went on lock down and I hated that. Being on lock down for something you had nothing to do with was tough. Apparently this was the norm down here. If you're not paired up next to your walking mate, they would turn you around or walk you to SEG.

To me SEG was just another part of the jail. No matter where you were you were still incarcerated. Again you have to have a strong mindset for the games these people played. They loved dangling the word fear in your face seeing if you were going to be afraid. See prison was designed to reprogram your mind, break your spirit and use your body as free labor. It was all about control.

Months had passed by and I had to find a way to escape Pinckneyville. I just couldn't do it anymore. Out of all the prisons I visited, this one by far was the worst. It was a black hole that you were forced to live in. My mother had come down yesterday and she brought my son and my nieces Kendra and Tanisha. I haven't seen my loved ones in years. It was a bittersweet moment, because I couldn't leave with them. My eyes were giving me trouble and I was having headaches. My mother asked if there was something wrong with my eyes. I told her no. I didn't want her worrying. She said a lady told her something was wrong with my eyesight. I was astonished and I when glanced at the woman who was seated at a round table near the back of the room, it looked as though she was praying for me.

I acknowledged her with a head nod and she beamed brightly as her lips continue to talk in silence. I could still see her aging light colored skin glowing. She wore her gray hair slicked back in a bun. I felt a little uncomfortable and tried to shake her off. Because the devil could bless you too, I questioned everything and trusted nothing.

January 22, 2009 2:13 A.M.

Kindly Advice

Listen, prison ain't where it's at.

Too many Cats were wearing too many hats.

Going bare back when that book bag carries nothing but facts.

Some say they're clean but I've seen many things and clean wasn't one of them.

The bars can keep you trapped but it's up to you to find a way to free yourself.

The joke is on you, you're the human zoo.

The prodigal son has returned home.

The Masta is delighted a feast is prepared.

Everybody eats, and everybody drinks.

But tomorrow there will be nothing but sorrow and you

my friend will be stuck searching for a better tomorrow.

Don't get it twisted.

Prison ain't where it's at.

I had a little over 4 years left on my remaining sentence and these years couldn't fly by any faster. I continued to write to keep myself busy and to stay out the way. I couldn't put in for a transfer until 3 more months. I still wanted out of this black hole. I noticed ever since the old lady prayed for me my eyes were feeling fine. There was no more pain.

Yes God was truly amazing He had His hand on me and I will be forever grateful. He has shown me miracles right in front of my own eyes, can't nobody tell me nothing about Jesus. I remember once I was having chest pains and the pain was so intense and unbearable. I said, "In the Blood of Jesus please take this pain." Seconds later, the pain was gone. Again I was truly amazed by the power of God. Prayer works and its true His love is everlasting.

In prison, joy is like a good stiff drink. Once the buzz is gone the pain returns. I had a celly I was not getting along with. He was a dark and gloomy fellow that rubbed people the wrong way. He stood 5ft 7in and weighed about 155 lbs. He was as light as a feather. I was like straight water and he was greasier than a can of oil. We did not mix. He worshiped Satan and I rocked with God. So there was a conflict brewing each and every day. It was powerful. This guy was a snake and I had to find a way to cut his head off without harming him. We should agree to disagree; not want to kill each other. In a world that makes sense that would be plausible.

I could feel my spirit being attacked it was exhausting and at times I was losing my patience. But I was trying to do everything in my power not to go upside his head. One day, I was lying in my bunk asleep and I felt the bed jerk. I looked up and my celly was using the bathroom taking a leak. But I know my eyes were not deceiving me.

“Man I know damn well you’re not standing up in here butt naked?” I screamed leaping from my bunk.

“What I’m a man.”

I didn’t waste any time as my fist of fury started to fly. Tonight it was time for the Devil and I to dance. The old suit was back on and it always seemed to fit perfectly. I was placed back in SEG. Later that night two White Shirts came to my cell. Basically they were patting me on my back for taking care of one of their huge problems. They promised to make sure they go easy on me at the hearing. I wasn't paying them know mind I was more upset with myself for allowing this clown to stress me out for so long. Stress is a silent killer and I tried to stay clear of it. I sat in my thoughts thinking about the loved ones I lost. Grandma Rose with her strength and feistiness. Grandma Ann with her unconditional love and long conversations. My uncle Maurice had passed and now my Grandfather William Sullivan, may he also rest in paradise. I couldn't attend their home-going celebrations due to my circumstances so I had to grieve in my own way.

The Pen

I couldn't stop pacing the walls of my hell.

The pen wanted to talk I wanted to yell.

Deep in thought, I'm a beast in the dark.

Shadows that gave chase were going to have come a lot harder.

Trouble Waters I see you, you just won't leave. Will you?

The waters are getting high.

I gotta grab a life coat to keep afloat.

Is death a friend or foe? Tell me do you know?

Why should we love something we know one day we will lose?

Nothing is ever promised, but a grave and a new pair of shoes.

READY FOR THE WORLD

The struggle within is probably the greatest challenge man will ever experience. The road to failure is paved with excessive pleasure, but dark sorrow will be waiting for you at the end of the journey. I think the only reason why men fail is broken focus. I had learned a lot about myself over the long years. About who I was as a person and what I was made out of. Something's I found out disappointed me and I used that disappointment to motivate me to change what I did not like.

I threw out everything I found rotten and replaced those items with something that was healthier. Patience was one. We want what we want now! One lesson prison will teach you is patience. Nothing moves without their command. Everything in prison you had to wait on. Food. Yard. Gym. Commissary. Medical. Shower. Phone. Patience is virtue in order to survive you have to have it. There was no other way around it. The ability to wait for something without getting angry or upset is a valuable quality in a person. I wanted to be a better man once I walked outside these walls. I wanted to be free in the mind and pure in desire. I wanted to be more understanding and not quick to judge. Not quick to get angry and resort to violence. For the first time in my life I felt like I had a chance to succeed. I had a game plan all I had to do now was go out there and execute it. I was never shy on confidence, but doubt always took up a resident in the back of my mind.

When you are posed to do something epic everybody is not going to be receptive to your vision. I had a lot of dream stealers always telling me what I couldn't do, but seldom ever told me what I could do. I was learning friends and so called brothers, weren't friends or so called brothers. I had to surround myself with new people who believed in me and wanted to see me genuinely prosper. I like the notion of rockin' with 4 solid quarters in my pockets rather than a hundred shiny pennies.

I had 2 years left on the remainder of my sentence and I was more than ready for the world. People always ask what is the first thing you're going to do when you get out? I always give the same answer "God willing, Breathe." But at the same time I'm going to enjoy life to the fullest. I'm coming for everything they said I could not have. Just because they said I could not have it.

I can't stop the pouring Black Rain from coming down. But I will be damned if I sit back and let it wet me up again. God has given me a vision and it is up to me to go out there and live it.

Months were falling off the calendar in a hurry it was summer already. I had one more freakin' summer to give them and I was done. I got my final summary back from the US District Courts yesterday. They finally put the dagger in me. For over 2 years I've been battling the Federal Government and Lisa Madigan's office. I was once told my case wouldn't make it out of an Appellate courtroom. I made it to each branch of Government all by myself. Now I had exhausted my last remedies so I had no more room to fight. I was like a fish dead in the water. Was I disappointed? Of course.

All I wanted was a fair hearing and couldn't get that. No money? No fair shot. These were the real breaks. A man without proper resources wasn't supposed to win. I fought these people for 12 long years and lost every round. However, I learned every fight that you have you don't necessarily have to win. But you gotta fight. Win, lose, or draw; you fight. *That's what Grandma Rose, taught me.* And that is the concept you have to apply to your everyday life. When the going gets tough you can't sit in the middle of the street and pout traffic doesn't stop, you must keep moving.

****

Everything was everything. I continued to hold my head up as I walked through the fire. Something dramatic was going on in the prison. Chow lines were being turned around. Inmates were ordered to lock down immediately. *What now? This place was like Comedy Central.* Personally I didn't care what was going on I was so ready to leave this camp.

My celly comes in the cell and he was mad at the world. No chow for a hungry man will leave his stomach in knots.

"Man these people are bogus down here. We can't go a week without a lock down. Knowing I didn't go to the store this week," he huffed climbing up in the bunk.

A man must learn to prepare himself for, "what if's." Some of these men in here couldn't think pass go, so you know they were not going to be collecting two hundred dollars. However this wasn't the game of Monopoly. It's not what you have; it's what you can keep. A man has to put a nest egg away for a raining day. It's basic common sense. If you're not paying attention you will get lost in the shuffle. Over the years, I had the opportunity to mentor a lot of young men who came to me openly wanting a drink from the cup of knowledge to quench their thirst.

I taught them what self-worth was. If you don't love yourself, you won't go far in the game. On many of occasions I had stuck my neck out there to help transform these young boys into men. I didn't care what gang they belong to. You were a man before anything. Dr. Maya Angelo said, "If you know better you do better." She was right and we the people must all do better.

We were on level one lock down and nobody knew what was going on until we saw armed riflemen on rooftops. The local news was live outside the prison. An inmate had kidnapped the librarian and held a sharp weapon to her throat. Everything was playing out live on a local TV station. I had a bad feeling this wasn't going to end well. Five hours had passed then all of a sudden you heard a loud explosion that sounded like someone was shooting off some fireworks. We were watching the news and they confirmed the hostage standoff was over. The inmate was shot and killed by the Illinois State Troopers.

From my understanding all the man wanted was more library time to work on his appeal case. This was my reality of hell I was living in. It takes a strong man to walk in the storm. This man gave up out of frustration and the storm swept him away. This lock down lasted for three weeks, but it didn't take long for something else to go wrong. Four days late I was returning from the yard, our housing unit was flooded with cops and medical staff members.

Immediately, the joint was placed on another level one lock down. I was livid because I just did 6 months now. Every other month I was locked down again. In prison, the little time you have away from your cell or cellmate was vital for your peace of mind. A man has to be able to hear himself think.

One by one in handcuffs, they called us down to answer their questions. *Where were you yesterday? Did you see anything unusual? Do you know anything? If you know something we advise you to tell us. You know we can make your life a living hell.* Although I knew exactly what they were looking for, but when you're in prison somebody else's business is the last thing you should be speaking on. If it didn't involve you, your eyes looked the other way.

An inmate had been found dead in his cell and all hell had broken loose. I guess people, wasn't telling fast enough, because they cut off the power in the housing unit. I was a seasoned vet, a real convict and I was used to the extreme tactics these people would use to get you to comply. I remember being locked down in Shawnee prison. We went without running water for a week. The toilets were backed up and you could smell stench of human waste everywhere. Food trays would be late purposely. Temperatures were extremely hot. It was by far a horrible experience. Again this was a part of the games these people played. They had the advantage and there was nothing you could do but file a prison grievance. However most of those grievances went nowhere. A news reporter reported a story of a man finding hundreds of prison grievance from inmates on the side of the road. So that tells you what these people think of an inmate grievance.

Federal and state laws govern the establishment and administration of prisons as well as the rights of the inmates. Although prisoners do not have full Constitutional rights, they are protected by the Constitutional's prohibition of cruel and unusual punishment. It's important for a man to know what he's up against. The problem I had with prisons was I knew they weren't any better than the jurisdictional system. They both were notorious at violating your Constitutional rights.

A few more days had passed by and miraculously the power came back on and the smoke was clear. Three Latino inmates were now facing first degree murder charges. They violated a member of their gang. He suffered from internal bleeding and died in his sleep. It was sad for all parties involved. I knew the kid very well. I was his barber. He would always say, "Cooley I need that cut. I got a visit coming this Saturday." Yeah, I'm going to miss my little dude. But what man has to realize is he, himself, has the power to choose his own fate. Your actions dictate your future. We got to move with extreme caution. I was lucky, I was bold and reckless running through life with no regards. I thank the most High my God for opening my eyes, now I can see. I pray for the man who is lost and can't find his way home. May his eyes be able to see the man God intends for him to be.

There were so many unspeakable things that could happen to you in prison and the last thing you wanted to see is someone losing their life. I was drained and frustrated at the same time no matter how mentally strong I was. Your mental strength will be tested often. I couldn't afford to invest my mental energy on unproductive thoughts. There's nothing wrong with tolerating discomfort. You just couldn't let your emotions control you. That was something I was getting better at.

WHEN I GET FREE

You never know how strong you are until strong is your only option left standing.

February 25, 2012

Anticipation got me waiting to explore the joy of a new world.

To be subdued by its passions with childlike eyes.

All my life I looked for you.

My heart flutters like that of a first kiss.

Emotions that run deep are in the lines of my face.

Don't leave your footprints if you don't plan on staying.

My winters have been too cold.

I'm waiting for spring.

Seeds are planted, in the summer they will bloom.

I had 12 months and 13 days left. Pinckneyville was still trying to hold me hostage. For months, I had been taking drug classes and any other class I could take to inch my way out the door. My weight had bloomed to 245 pounds and trusts me; it was not a good look. My back arms looked like an old lady at bingo night waving *bingo*. My chest looked like I had breast implants. When I sat down to tie my shoe I was laboring heavily. I started eating one meal a day and worked out as often as I could. The weight came off and I started looking like myself again.

"Hey Cooley you have a visit," a white male C.O said, opening up my door.

"Okay, give me 10 minutes. Thank you," I replied.

Visit?

I wasn't expecting a visit, but it was probably my nieces Kendra and Nisha. I quickly reached into to my box and pulled out my crispy blue outfit. You always wanted to looked fresh and clean when you were headed up top to the visiting area. You wanted to show your love ones all was well. When I got there this tall thin white female officer led me to a table in the rear of the visiting room. She had very nasty attitude I could careless for.

Fifteen minutes had gone by, then thirty minutes. I was sitting there looking crazy while everybody else was sitting enjoying their visitors. A black woman at the next table told me they had turned two young ladies and a little boy away. I signaled for the white female officer.

She was watching me the whole time. “Excuse me ma’am can I have a word with you?” I asked politely.

The lines in her forehead deepen and her face twisted in a frown. She rose to her feet and headed in my direction. Her narrow hips swayed from side to side.

“You can return to your housing unit. Your visit has been terminated,” she said coldly.

“Terminated? Excuse me what happen?”

“Their names were not on your list. Now go!”

“Ma’am that doesn’t make any sense their names has always been on my visitor’s list,” I stated.

She quickly turned on her heels and her big brown eyes shot two daggers at me. “I could care less. I can make sure your visiting privileges will be suspended for 6 months,” she yelled.

The room fell silent and all eyes were on the Serpent. I didn’t know what had clawed up this lady’s pants leg, but she was on the verge of getting cussed out. With fire rising in my eyes I ran a cool hand through my short crop hair. *Lawd. Why change gotta be so hard?* It took everything inside of me to turn and walk away. My pride took a hit as I made the walk of shame all the way back to my housing unit. My anger was rising with each step. As soon as I got back, I asked to see a white shirt. Something had to be done to this chick. She was foul.

Lt. Johnson came to talk to me. He was a short bubbly man who kinda resembled Barney Rubble from the Flintstones. Unlike some Lt's this guy cared and he followed the book accordingly. I respected that. After a long conversation, he ensured me the female officer would be dealt with. I was sitting on my bunk listening to Mary J. Blige sing her heart out on the My Life album. Her album and Carl Thomas's Emotional album were two of my favorite. Music helped chase the blues away. It gave life to the spirit. Moments later, my cell door flew open and four officers had walked in.

"Stand up Harris you're going to SEG."

"SEG? For what?"

"You know what you did, on your feet now," A short stocky C.O. with a full red beard sneered.

"I can't pack my property?"

"It will get packed for you. Turn around and put your hands behind your back," red beard ordered.

See this is the hell a man has to endure when he puts himself in harm's way. When I got over to SEG and I read my charges I was hotter than hell. This chick claimed I had threatened her and made degrading sexual remarks. Here we go again. More lies and deceit, she even had another officer co-signing her story. For the next two days, I racked my brain trying to come up with a plan. All I had was the truth on my side and in my case most of time that didn't mean anything. Here I was trying to do the right thing instead of the wrong thing and somehow I still came out on the bottom. *Explain that to me Oh Lord, I cried out.*

A man that has hate in his heart is a man that is walking around with a time bomb strapped to his chest. It won't be long before the bomb goes off. Hate is a strong word and I was trying my best to move that negative energy out of my life. But when something we don't like happens to fall in our laps that hate can become real again. I was not going to take an L on this lying down. I'm a fighter and I was ready to fight.

Last night I sat down with my pen and wrote a long letter to Internal Affairs. Normally I don't mess with those people but this is the only card I had left to play so I played it. I was hoping my writing skills would be able lure the big boys from behind the desk. I had only one shot left in the chamber so I had to make it count. Yeah they got down dirty on me, but what they didn't know was I had a friend in the pen.

The pen has been my friend for some years now. If it were not for the pen, I probably wouldn't be still breathing. The pen had a way of turning a bad situation into a positive one because the pen always tried to find the good in a bad situation. When I wanted to jump off the edge, the pen always brought me back. He was my voice of reasoning when I could not think for myself.

"Hey, you got a visit?"

Visit? It had to be passed midnight. It had to be them people.

I was ushered into a small room without any windows. A large white man with grey hair sat behind a desk. He was a Lieutenant. He gave me permission to sit with a wave of a hand, then jarred back in the chair placing his folded beefy hands behind his head.

"Look I don't know what I can do for you. I thought I would come by and see you because you did make some valid points in your argument. You have very good writing skills. I must say it did peak my interest. Again I can't promise you anything, but I will take a peek into it.

I gave him a long piercing look before I was seated. "I appreciate you coming down. Like I said in the letter, if I did what she said I did. The cameras would show it."

"Why do you think she would make up a story like this?"

I paused leaning forward to gather my thoughts. “Some people are so angry with their own lives. They will do anything to torment someone else’s life. I left the visiting room at 2:25 pm. If she felt threatened, and was so distraught like she claimed. Why wait to write up a report at 10:45 pm. If someone took a shot at me, I’m not going to wait 6 hours and then call the police. My guess is Lt. Johnson went over there, scolded her, and now she was seeking revenge. I am on transfer to Big Muddy any day. This is a ploy to ruin my transfer. All you have to do is call down the witnesses who were there in the visiting room. Cameras don’t lie when the smoke clears she should be reprimanded. What she’s doing is unprofessional.”

The Lt. stood up and shook my hand. “For what it’s worth I’m sorry. I know I’m not supposed to say this, but I do believe you. I also think she’s trying to sabotage your transfer. Like I said I can’t promise you anything but I will shake some trees.”

I returned back to my cage feeling optimistic. I can only hope the truth comes out in my favor. The next day I was being moved to the other side of the wing. I was being placed in a cell with a celly. As soon as the door swung open, I observed an older brown skin brother lying asleep on the bottom bunk. He stirred long enough to introduce himself as Tony aka “Teo.” Right away I could tell Teo and I would get along well. We talked for hours laughing and joking like we had known each other our entire lives. Tony was a Gangster, a real OG.

He was smart and humble and had compassion for others. But if you cross that line, he will bite your head off.

The days were flying by and the more I talked and listen to Teo, I knew I was here in this cell for a reason. God don't make mistakes. Teo was living the lifestyle I wanted. I saw my blueprint in him. He had the queen, the big house, and his own small business. I'm not going to lie I was inspired and the more he talked, the more I listened. I shared with Teo some of the stories I had been writing and he too wanted to write a book. He let me see an unfinished manuscript about his life story he had been working on. I gave him a few pointers and showed him how to put seasoning on his word play to make the book more enjoyable. I thought the book was good and I was pleased to give him some assistance.

They dropped all charges and gave me two weeks in SEG. I heard the female officer had been placed in the tower. This was part of her punishment. If you asked me, she should've been suspended without pay. However, they did see the cameras and talked to three witnesses who all confirmed my story. Normally in this dark underworld the truth does not get a chance to see the light. Had I not had a friend in the pen things would've probably went south. When I get free I told Teo we are going to kick it like players. Smoke big cigars and enjoy life. The cage is no place for a man who was going places. Yep, when I get free the world will know me.

I'M COMING HOME

If you step outside in the night, you can hear the world sleeping.

You can even hear a few snorts.

But what you don't see is that burning melting pot in its core.

The wind sings tunes you've never heard before.

Does this mean there's something wrong?

Life is too short for loathing.

Some storms come from beneath your skin.

Rough road maps are hard to follow.

But if you want to win you have to look within.

March 28, 2012

It was 10 am and I had just arrived at Big Muddy Correctional Center in Ina Illinois. God is good. I prayed I would be in another joint on my birthday. Today is my birthday and it will be the last birthday I had behind bars. I didn't believe in celebrating my birthday in prison. I had conditioned my mind long ago birthdays and holidays was just another day on the calendar. I had to move forward, because when you are moving forward you see different things every day. When you are moving backwards you keep seeing the same things.

Big Muddy prison was something else, I seen a lot of crazy things in prisons but Big Muddy took it to another level. This prison held a majority of sex offenders. It was like their safe haven. I came here for their drug program that was the only way I could transfer out of Pinckneyville. I heard a lot of strange fruits were down here. But to see them close up it was mind blowing. My first celly was a tall white guy with blond hair. He was known as the Baby Raper. So my words to him were short. Being around some of these creeps were giving me the heebie jeebies. I sat in meetings all day and listened to pedophiles tell their stories. This was not my crowd and I was not the one to stay silent. I knew once I opened my mouth and spoke the truth, they were going to kick me out the program.

Personally, I thought the program was a joke and some of these worthless souls needed to be castrated. This was a buddy system to keep the sex offenders to together to help them do their bid comfortably. If you had a problem with them, you will be removed quickly. Here, they were protected. I saw so many high profile sex offenders that I read about or seen on TV. The he/she's were everywhere, but the problem down here was you didn't know who was who. Everybody was suspect. I saw a guy who could lift every weight in the gym then come back to the cell block and be somebody else's old lady. No matter how much time I had to do, I could never get use to this life. I trusted no one and watched everybody.

Months had flown by and I think my days were numbered over in the Zoo. But I didn't care. I told my guy Twain I was ready to move around. Twain was probably the only guy I respected in the joint. He was a tall slim brother from Alton, Illinois. Twain was a true baller on the basketball court. When we played together, we were like Jordan and Pippen. Of course I was Jordan, but nevertheless we made the game fun. After Twain left and went home I mostly kept to myself, because in a place like this it's hard to find someone who you could bounce your ideas off of and call them a friend.

The number one question I get is, how did you do all that time? I tell them I had no choice. When you're backed into a corner trying to stay alive you fight. Basic instincts kicked in despite all the madness swirling around my head. I did meet a couple of decent brother's. Besides Twain I can't forget my right hand man Marvin (MG). Now this tall brown skin brother was a smooth cat. I was his barber and we went at it on the basketball court. In prison it was something about the basketball court, a place where special bonds of friendship were made. The love of the game doesn't leave your heart no matter how dark the road you travel. MG was like a younger brother and I had a lot of love for him. After I leave, he will have 6 more years to give before his out date. I told him no worries; I am my brother's keeper. I was going to rock with him to the end. *I gotcha!*

December 18, 2012

This morning I woke up being moved to a new cell block. I couldn't hide the huge Kool aid smile that covered my face. They finally went behind my back and had me removed from the program. I wanted to know what took them so long. *The brother with the conscience mind is gone carry on.* I wanted to scream in elation. I guess when people see you are outspoken and self-reliant they view you as a threat. However, I refuse to dumb down to get along, just to get along. I will speak my mind and stand up for what I believe in. A man that doesn't stand for something, he will fall for anything. In prison, there were a lot males but there were very few men.

Lesson learned. A man cannot be defined by his definition. His character and his integrity defined who he is. Being a man was tough but being a black man was even tougher. You had to work much harder than the next man and that always bothered me. I believe a man should be able to stand on his merits. He shouldn't be judged by the color of his skin nor his creed. I saw so much racism and unfairness in my lifetime. It hurts sometimes just to think about it. Black people are not making excuses for our circumstances we just want a level playing field. I never wanted anybody to give me anything. Just like James Brown said point me to the door and I'll get it myself.

Even though my time was winding down, I felt numb to the feeling of being released. I don't know how to explain it. I thought I would be going crazy towards the end of my bid; excited out of my mind. But surprisingly, I felt even keeled. I was going out into the world as a new me. The old self as far as I was concerned died back in Pittsburgh. I was ready to out-work, out-hustle, out live and out eat everything moving. I was hungrier than a Mountain Lion. The energy inside of me was ready to burst. I was focused, focused more than I had ever been before. It was time to take another shot at life and this time failure was not an option.

March 25, 2013

I was up early praising God, blessed to see this day. The journey had been long and at times overwhelming. Last night the guys gave me a home going celebration. I have taken part in so many of these celebrations now it was my turn. Funny thing was I still had to cook the meal, because no one could out cook me. I won't miss prison but I will miss some of the guys who are good men but made poor choices. I always say never make a mistake you can't come back from. These guys are counting on me to go out here and live, not just for me, but also for them too. I met a guy who got sentenced to 150 years. He said, "With your brain there's no reason why you shouldn't be rich." The guys in prison were by far the smartest people I have ever met. If anybody would've told me 20 years ago I would be in prison today, I would've laughed at them. That just goes to show you when it's dark outside, it's hard to see the road.

Prison life is like a slow death, every day they shoot you in the vein with poison to see how long you are going to last. Sadly, some of the guys in here won't make it to the finish line. If they do survive, mentally they're dead. It takes a rare breed to come inside these walls and battle these demons head up and walk out in one piece. Two nights ago, I had a dream that left me shook. My stepfather (Bubba) had come to me in a vision and he was explaining to me how to get assistance from Government Agencies who will help excons. That was typical of Bubba he was always on top of things. His last words, was take care of your brother (Frank).

Immediately, I jolted upright from my sleep, palms sweating my feet were cold. For a minute I didn't know where I was, the dream felt so real. Every dream I have I always try to analyze its meaning. Because I am a firm believer we have dreams for a reason. When I was younger I used to always have this odd dream. In the dream I would be deep in an ocean surrounded by sharks swimming in this huge circle. Every time I would try to leave the circle, the sharks attacked me. Deep waters, was something I feared, the sharks were there to feast if I got outside my body.

The air was cold against my face as I was being escorted to the front gate. An officer made small talk as he held paper work in his hand. It was three of us being released. Finally my day has arrived. My family was waiting for me on other side of the wall. This was a divine moment and every step I took my feet pounded the pavement with purpose. My head was held high, just like the first day when I walked into this house of hell. 13 years and 6 months, 4,472 days, 142 months and 11,424 hours.

I gave these people a part of me I will never be able to get back. That hurts in itself and I know I will have to live with that pain for the rest of my life. However, I can't stop the black rain from falling outside my window and I can't say it will never wet me up again. But what I can say is I am now equipped with the tools to minimize the consumption and filter the effects the black rain has on my mind, body and spirit.

I AM

I refuse to hang my head in a sad place.

The gift of life is worth living.

So why aren't you living?

Depression leaves a bad taste in my mouth that

I can live without.

But lemme, tell you something I will never regret.

Being born black, a man is who I am.

I stand strong like a mighty Lion ready to do battle.

I spread my mighty wings like an Eagle and soar the skies.

When I spit you can hear the very essence of my ancestors speak.

Even though the color of my skin rubs people the wrong way,

I am proud of the eumelanin that makes my dark skin unique.

I am proud of my full lips that God made with his fingertips.

I am proud to be blessed beyond measures that no man can protest.

Almost 14 years ago I watched my world fall apart.

That was day my freedom, she left me and broke my heart...

My life never mattered to some and it never will.

But when I look in the mirror I see a man that didn't sell

his soul and that is real.

I am who I am.

OUTRO

Just before my grandfather William Sullivan had passed. We were engaged in a heartfelt conversation over the phone. He had asked, "why was I continuing to ruin my life with foolishness? When are you going to straighten up and fly right?" I responded blaming everything and everybody else for my circumstances. He angrily raised his voice abruptly cutting me off and gave me a resounding ear spitting verbal assault. To say the least, I was beyond shocked because my grandfather had never raised his voice or laid a finger on me my entire life.

My granddad was a warm gentle giant who stood strong and proud. He was branded in integrity and character. When he walked, into a room his presence automatically demanded respect. So I listened attentively to the sound of his voice. He was weak at the time; battling old age and illnesses. His frail voice strained to almost a harsh whisper eagerly trying to muster up enough strength to rattle my cage. I knew he was deeply disappointed in me and subsequently that had crushed me. From that day forward I made a teary eyed oath that I would get myself together. Sadly, that was the last conversation we had 2 weeks later he died.

Even to this day, I still keep my granddad's words etched in my heart. Although every day I rise, it still remains a struggle to stay motivated and positive in an unjust world. The positive energy that I daily surround myself with helps fuel a healthy excursion in my life, that keeps my feet rooted in disciple. This book goes out to the young men who may find themselves engulfed in painful elements, struggling to survive in a poor stricken environment saturated with senseless violence. Where vulnerability of negative energy surrounds them regularly like deadly land mines.

My only hope is you can find inspiration to never give up no matter how rough the road may become. Success is within you. *But the question is how bad do you want it? And how hard are you willing to work for it?* I can only speak from my perspective on what I perceive or know from first hand experiences. Experience has a way of being a good teacher. Over the years, I have looked into the complicated eyes of so many young black men. I see an absence of hope and courage that flutters deep within. I see so much potential, but they lack the faith or patience it takes to endure the difficult tides that challenge our daily lives.

I see a lot of young men falling into different cliques or small groups they feel comfortable with. Instead of pulling together as one to make a difference; like so many other past generation of black men did. These men stood up, fought, and died for freedom, equality and injustice so all men of color could achieve the American Dream. And what are we doing to repay them for their ultimate sacrifice? Nothing, but killing each other and committing self-genocide.

For some strange reason we take great joy and pride in self-hatred reinforcing the crab-in-a-barrel mentality. Some tend to give up too soon and go astray. Other's fall deep into depression, abusing alcohol and drugs then dive head first into a sea of crime to feed the angered power of our demons.

As the sands of time continue to tick forward we find ourselves lost in the chaos of disparity blaming life for being unfair to us. But in reality we were unfair to life. No one ever promised us life was going to be untroublesome. In fact, life requires a great amount of energy to stay alive. God blessed the black man with many gifts that set us apart. But essentially it falls on us. We have to man up and stop making excuses. So what the deck is stacked against us; it is what it is. If you don't like something, change it. We can't keep crying foul, life is a contact sport. You're going to get hit.

These are crazy times we are living in. You must stay vigilant and keep one eye open. Even when everything is crumbling around you must stay solid and focused. Never stop dreaming and when you find out who you are. You won't need someone to tell you.

4 YEARS LATER

Time doesn't stand still for no man. Unfortunately I had to find that out the hard way. These 4 years have flown by like a 747 jet. However, I can't complain because life is good. I'm breathing. My first 6 months out was tough but I was able to steer the ship in the right direction. I stuck to the blueprint and all the pieces began to come together. I have always been a hard worker so I was no stranger to the process. When you're starting from the bottom with nothing, the mountain is a steep hill to climb. I took the bad with the good and also took a few lumps working dead end jobs for low pay.

Finally I got smart and went back to doing what I did best, cleaning cars. Detailing cars was something I absolutely loved. There's nothing like taking something that once was and restoring it to make it look good again. I knew at this moment I was going to own a car detailing business. But how, was the question.

In March of 2015 I released my first novel "Deadly Betrayal." I was excited like a child at Christmas; this was my first creation being released into the world. This was a major accomplishment in my eyes; I achieved something I dreamed I would do. The book got rave reviews and I knew I was doing what I was supposed to be doing. It's a beautiful thing to be able to find your passion. The inner voice that couldn't be heard, people are now starting to listen.

January 6, 2016 I had neck surgery to repair a torn disc that was touching my spine. This was major surgery. If I didn't have this surgery it was a strong possibility I could become paralyzed. I prayed on it. I knew God didn't bring me this far to let me go. After the surgery, with excruciating pain shooting all through my body, the very next day I walked out of the hospital with my loving wife by my side. She is a great teammate, when the game is on the line she in there fighting beside me. When things don't look good her smile makes it all better. I didn't waddle in the mud and feel sorry for myself. Once again I had to find strength to pick myself up off the floor and keep it moving. With the love and support of my family the comeback was now even more special.

In this life, I had made terrible mistakes and poor decisions but God granted me a second chance at life and I will be forever indebted. It is because of His Amazing Grace that I stand strong today as a Homeowner, Small Business Owner, Writer, Poet, Motivational Speaker and a published Author. This is my 3rd book in 3 years. The journey has been special and I'm humble. Of course none of this would be possible without the Angel God sent to me from Heaven. Yes, I found my Queen and I married her (September 3, 2016). A man cannot conquer the world without a strong woman by his side. This woman is incredible, the joy of my life. She accepted my flaws and all my scars. I couldn't have asked for a better soul mate. To my beautiful butterfly, Jocelyn Harris, woman you are a blessing. (Love you)

Sixteen years ago I read a book that changed my life, *A Breed Apart*. I told myself once I was released I was going to find Mr. Victor Woods. Well it didn't take long. My first year out I tracked him down in Madison Wisconsin where he was the keynote speaker. We formed a bond of good friendship and I'm proud to say this brother has been a very powerful influential person in my life. Getting a front row seat watching him do what he enjoys motivates me to work even harder.

My goal is simple; keep pushing. I will continue to Live Love Life and let the wind propel against my backside. If I fall I will fall forward. You can't be afraid to fail. Scrapes and bruises go hand in hand with success. Many people are going to hate you because you're doing something extraordinary they can't do. Family will even hate you. Don't get discouraged. stick to the plan and go out there and make things happen for you.

God didn't make me mediocre so I won't pretend that He did. One of the worst fears I had to overcome was self-doubt. You can't accomplish anything if you don't try it. I think the smartest decision I've ever made in my life was to invest in myself. My motto is; *don't just dream a dream, live it.* If you can see in your mind there's no reason why you can't make it happen. *Be resilient... Be fearless... Be successful...*

Made in the USA
Lexington, KY
31 October 2017